Lord, I'M BROKEN

90-DAY
DEVOTIONAL

Lord, I'M BROKEN

90-DAY DEVOTIONAL

Carolyn Rice

REDEMPTION
PRESS

Published by Redemption Press, PO Box 427, Enumclaw, WA 98022
Toll Free (844) 2REDEEM (273-3336)

Redemption Press is honored to present this title in partnership with the author. The views expressed or implied in this work are those of the author. Redemption Press provides our imprint seal representing design excellence, creative content and high quality production.

Unless otherwise noted, all Scripture verses are from the Holy Bible, New King James Version®, nkjv® Copyright © 1979, 1980, 1982 by Thomas Nelson, Inc., Publishers. Used by permission.

Stock Photos Purchased from:
www.shutterstock.com

Credit/Attribution for Print:
© Shutterstock / Jumnian Pelt
© Shutterstock / PKpix
© Shutterstock / Yakira_photo
© Shutterstock / PhIllStudio

Designer: Brittany Osborn

ISBN 13: 978-1-68314-083-2 (Print)
        978-1-68314-084-9 (ePub)
        978-1-68314-085-6 (Mobi)

Library of Congress Catalog Card Number: 2016943507

Contents

Day 1: Take This Broken Life 1
Day 2: A Beautiful Reminder. 3
Day 3: Trust in the Middle of the Storm 5
Day 4: Remember His Love. 7
Day 5: Receive His Love 9
Day 6: The Beautiful Work in You. 11
Day 7: A New Identity. 13
Day 8: A Key to Freedom 15
Day 9: A Key to Daily Strength 17
Day 10: Peace in the Middle of the Storm. 19
Day 11: One More Day 21
Day 12: He Thinks You're Beautiful 23
Day 13: Keep It from Slipping Away. 25
Day 14: Making It a Habit. 27
Day 15: A Dangerous Root 29
Day 16: Realize His Love for You 31
Day 17: Your Healing Is Coming. 33
Day 18: Strength to Hold On. 35

Day 19: You Are Not Hopeless 37
Day 20: Grumbling Costs 39
Day 21: He Hears Your Cry 41
Day 22: Making a Choice 43
Day 23: Finding Comfort and Strength 45
Day 24: How Do I Get Joy? 47
Day 25: It's Time to Break the Chains 49
Day 26: Look Up 51
Day 27: You Are Loved 53
Day 28: From Broken to Beautiful 55
Day 29: Paid in Full 57
Day 30: Hold on to Your Dream 59
Day 31: Never Too Broken 61
Day 32: Speak Life 63
Day 33: Receive His Plan 65
Day 34: Seek His Face 67
Day 35: Rise Above 69
Day 36: Fear Not 71
Day 37: Give Him the Pain 73
Day 38: Shake It Out 75
Day 39: A Picture of Forgiveness 77
Day 40: Strength to Keep Going 79
Day 41: Rest in the Battle 81
Day 42: A Beautiful Mess 83
Day 43: A Quality Decision 85
Day 44: Victory over Negative Thoughts 87
Day 45: Giving Him Expectations 89
Day 46: Mind Protection 91
Day 47: Your Weapon 93
Day 48: A Picture of the Father 95

Day 49: Breaking the Power of the Past 97
Day 50: Permission to Feel 99
Day 51: He Knows Your Pain 101
Day 52: Strength through Praise 103
Day 53: A Peaceful Place 105
Day 54: Changing Your Mind 107
Day 55: God Has Not Forgotten You 109
Day 56: Healing Time 111
Day 57: Facing the Pain 113
Day 58: He Sees Your Tears 115
Day 59: Your Father Loves You 117
Day 60: God Believes in You 119
Day 61: The Whole Table 121
Day 62: Wiping Ugly Words Away 123
Day 63: A Reminder of His Goodness 125
Day 64: Keep Planting His Word 127
Day 65: Jesus Is Greater 129
Day 66: You Matter 131
Day 67: Hang On and Trust God 133
Day 68: Planting Words 135
Day 69: Freedom from Torment 137
Day 70: Sleep on It 139
Day 71: Why? 141
Day 72: Fill Your Cup 143
Day 73: Cling to Jesus 145
Day 74: Freedom from Manipulating Powers 147
Day 75: Daily Encouragement 150
Day 76: Healing from Depression 152
Day 77: Do You Love Me? 155
Day 78: The Way Out Is Through 157

Day 79: The Broken Pieces 159
Day 80: No More Torment 161
Day 81: Overcoming Doubt 163
Day 82: You Are Valuable 165
Day 83: Moving On. 167
Day 84: Who You Really Are. 169
Day 85: Yours to Keep. 171
Day 86: Practice Blessing. 173
Day 87: The Image in the Mirror 175
Day 88: Choose Life 177
Day 89: A Story 179
Day 90: Your Heart's Cry. 181

Author's Note 182

DAY 1

Take This Broken Life

To appoint unto them that mourn in Zion, to give unto
them beauty for ashes, the oil of joy for mourning, the
garment of praise for the spirit of heaviness; that they might
be called trees of righteousness, the planting of the Lord,
that he may be glorified.

—Isaiah 61:3 KJV

Would I always be broken?

Isolation wrapped itself around me. Lies and deceit
entangled themselves in my mind, and the biggest lie of all hindered
me from any friendship, making me feel alone in this world—the
lie that if I let people see me, really see me, they would reject me.
So I hid.

The gifts and talents God had placed in me lay buried in the
darkness of my soul, unable to come out.

I hid my true self in the dark and would not let her come
out. The person people saw on the outside was someone with no
emotion. I seldom spoke, and when I did, no one could hear what
I said because my voice was so quiet.

Underneath it all lay fear. Trauma and abuse had taught me
well. *Don't come out! You will get hurt!*

Often, insecurities arise when people are faced with an awkward
situation. Sitting with me, a person who would not talk to them or
barely even look them in the eye, became reason for some to think

this was about them in some twisted way. People's fears placed labels on me, and I found even more reason to hide.

But there was one who saw me. I could not hide from Him. He saw into the darkest places of my soul and loved me anyway.

He did not reject me but called me out of darkness and into His light. Instead of calling me ugly, hopeless, and of no account, He called me beautiful, beloved, and of great price in His kingdom.

He picked up each piece of my broken life and put me back together again.

There is someone you never have to hide from, someone who loves you very much and calls you into His light.

He is the healer of the broken.

He is the comforter of those who can only give Him their tears.

He will not leave you here.

You are not alone.

I have stood in the place you stand now, and I can tell you that our God is faithful.

Let Him gently draw you out. He wants to take the broken pieces of your life and make them into something beautiful.

He's calling you out. Will you answer?

You don't have to hide anymore.

PRAYER

Lord, I give you every broken piece of my life, and every tear I've ever cried. I lift them up to you, Lord, they are yours. Thank you that you are a God who gives beauty for ashes. And out of my brokenness, you will make something truly beautiful. I choose to trust that you are good. I receive your definition of me: beautiful, beloved, precious, and of great price. In Jesus' name, amen.

DAY 2

A Beautiful Reminder

I will sing of the mercies of the Lord forever: with my mouth I
will make known thy faithfulness to all generations.
—Psalm 89:1 KJV

T he invitation I held in my hand told a wonderful story.
A picture of a beautiful couple at their wedding fifty
years before adorned the front. They looked so young, their whole
lives ahead of them; and now, they were celebrating fifty years of
that life together. I was excited to celebrate with people who had
become so special to me.

During the celebration we watched a slideshow of pictures from
years gone by. Their children spoke of how their parents did not give
up when times were hard but instead trusted in God's faithfulness.
Every time, they saw God come through. He never let them down.

Just days before, I had cried my eyes out to the Lord, bringing
Him a heartbreaking situation. My husband and I had tried so
hard, done everything we could, and yet it seemed that things
were getting worse.

The Lord used this celebration to remind me not to give up
because He is faithful. I had not failed but was grieving the bad
choices of someone I loved. The battle would take place on my
knees in prayer. It was time to rely on the faithfulness of God and
put this person into His hands.

When you don't understand why things around you seem to be falling apart and going just the way you didn't want them to, remember God's love for you. Remember God's faithfulness. He will bring you through this storm with a testimony of His goodness, faithfulness, and love.

Someday we ourselves will look back on our own lives, telling others who have come after us about the beauty of God's faithfulness. Do not give up but continue moving forward, knowing God will come through for you.

PRAYER

Lord, thank you that you are faithful. Thank you that you will come through. Give me strength, Father, to not give up, but to continue to trust in your faithfulness. I choose not to sink into despair and hopelessness. I choose instead to trust in you, God, and to find comfort in your presence and in your Word. I ask for encouragement as I wait on you. In Jesus' name, amen.

DAY 3

Trust in the Middle of the Storm

Thus says the Lord to you: "Do not be afraid
nor dismayed because of this great multitude,
for the battle is not yours, but God's."
—2 Chronicles 20:15

In the stillness of the night, I willed my heart to quiet within me, but it wouldn't listen.

Without my permission, the tears escaped, rolling silently down my face toward my ears and onto the pillow. Even after they were gone, other tears, hot and wet, soon took their place. I couldn't stop them.

I rose from my bed, wiped the wetness from my face, and collected my journal.

Dim light settled across the page as my pen fashioned words that painted a picture of my pain. Every letter, every word was a release until I felt I could close the book and go to sleep.

My alarm clock announced morning too soon.

I usually awoke to it beeping. But this morning, words from a Christian station filled the room. "You can't trust the Lord for the current battles until you take the time to remember the battles He's already won."

Those words played in my mind all day, like a song I couldn't get out of my head. And all day I listed out battles that the Lord had already won. Instead of despair, I was filled with thankfulness.

I felt faith rise up within me, that what God had done before, He would do again.

When you are overwhelmed with discouragement and a broken heart has got you down, take just a moment and think on the things God has already done. It will change your focus from the situation to God and give you hope for the coming days.

PRAYER

Heavenly Father, I choose to trust you. I thank you that you have already won many battles on my behalf. You have brought me this far, and you will not leave me here. Thank you that you are a God who keeps your promises. In Jesus' name, amen.

DAY 4

Remember His Love

Blessed are they that mourn; for they shall be comforted.
—Matthew 5:4 KJV

During a quiet moment between worship and the sermon, my friend leaned close and whispered, "I have something for you."

She pressed a small, heart-shaped button into my hand, looked into my eyes, and said, "I want you to remember that God's love covers this situation. I just feel that everything's going to be alright."

Those were the words I needed to hear. Our family had lived through months of chaos. We were weary and heartbroken.

I put the heart button in my office where I would see it every day. It reminds me that when I was going through a hard time, God sent someone to encourage me.

When the waters are rocky and you feel discouraged and heartbroken, remember that God's love is with you in the middle of the storm. While it may rage around you, you are covered by the love of almighty God.

You are not walking through this storm alone.

What has happened to you will not be wasted.

In the midst of darkness and discouragement, declare that you know God loves you and that His love covers you in this storm. Rest in His love, declaring to the storm that your God is faithful.

You are right in the palm of your heavenly Father's hand, and you are covered by His love.

7

PRAYER

Father God, I choose to trust that you are a good father and that you have good in store for me. I will not always be walking through this, but you will turn my mourning into praise. I pray that you would send your encouragement and give me what I need to walk through one more day. In Jesus' name, amen.

DAY 5

Receive His Love

As the Father hath loved me, so have I loved you: continue ye
in my love.

—John 15:9 KJV

On my journey to healing, I struggled to forgive one person
in particular.

During the process, God showed me this person didn't know
how to love because they had not been loved themselves. It didn't
take away the hurt and pain but gave me a greater understanding
of why they did what they did.

And eventually, it helped me to fully forgive.

I had to come to terms with the fact that this person failed me
and that no other person on earth could give me back what was
stolen. Only Jesus could truly heal my heart.

I learned to look to God instead of other people to meet my
needs. And the love that I hadn't been able to find in others, I
found in Him.

I grew in the knowledge of His love, and as I began to believe
His love for me, it changed the way I felt about myself. I learned
to love myself and in turn, was better able to walk in love toward
others.

You can grow in the knowledge of God's love through His word.

When you come upon a verse about the love of your heavenly
Father, take that word for yourself, repeating it out loud. Memorize

that Scripture, getting it deep into your spirit, letting it change you from the inside out.

The truth of God's love for you will be planted in your heart for life.

PRAYER

Lord, I thank you that you love me so much that you sent Jesus to die on the cross, so I could have eternal life. Help me to see my own value in your eyes and to receive your love for myself. Help me to love myself and in turn, love others the way you would love them through me. In Jesus' name, amen.

DAY 6

The Beautiful Work in You

Being confident of this very thing, that he which hath begun a
good work in you will perform it until the day of Jesus Christ:
—Philippians 1:6 KJV

I was only putting stitches in fabric, but God was giving me a
picture of His work in me.

For months I worked to turn tiny stitches into a beautiful fabric
picture. I knew what it was *supposed* to look like from the pattern
I bought. But as I put more and more stitches in, it looked like a
big mess.

Over time, I slowly worked all the stitches together until finally,
the mess turned into something beautiful. I held up my creation
and framed it for everyone to see.

You may feel like a mess right now.

But if you will allow Him, God will work in your life.

He has a beautiful plan, and when He's done, your life will be
a lovely picture of the beauty He has worked in you.

Decide today that you will not give up and instead, you will
trust the Lord for the strength to walk through one more day.

The Lord is doing a beautiful work in you.

PRAYER

Father God, I give you the broken pieces of my life, and I thank you that nothing will be wasted. I trust that you will take the mess I give you and make it into something beautiful. I invite you to work in my heart and in my life. In Jesus' name, amen.

A New Identity

My soul melteth for heaviness: strengthen me according to
your word.
—Psalm 119:28 KJV

"I have heard your cries. I have seen your tears. I know your
sorrows and your sufferings, and I am coming to save you!"
The teacher's voice boomed across the room.

I wiped the tears from my eyes, head down, hoping no one
would see. Why had I sat in the front of the class that day?

Through prayer, I had felt led to go to Bible college, and
everything had come together for me to be there. I didn't consider
myself Bible college material. I was broken, wounded, and bruised
from the inside out. That had become my identity. But God was
about to take that from me and give me a new identity in Him.

Through my time in Bible college, the Lord gave me a love for
His word. It is time spent in the Word of God that helped me let
go of ungodly words spoken to me as a child. Those ugly words
have been replaced with God's truth.

The words others have spoken over you can take root in your
life. When you replace those words with the truth of God's Word,
you begin to develop new root systems and can grow into the
healthy person God created you to be.

Even as little as fifteen minutes a day in the Word on a consistent
basis can help change the way you think about yourself.

Spend some time in the Word of God today. Ask Him to give you understanding and to minister to you through His Word.

PRAYER

Father God, I pray that you would comfort me through your Word today. Teach me, Lord. I want to learn. Give me an understanding of your Word, and let it speak to my heart. Help me develop a habit of consistently being in your Word. In Jesus' name, amen.

DAY 8

A Key to Freedom

Then said Jesus, Father, forgive them; for they know not what
they do. And they parted his raiment, and cast lots.
—Luke 23:34 KJV

Everything in me wanted to run out of the room, yet I sat still.
"Why don't you want to forgive?" My counselor asked.

Hadn't she just heard what they did to me?

I couldn't answer her right away. At the thought of forgiving
those who abused me, a ball of emotions, all jumbled and mixed
together, welled up within my chest: resistance, anger, bitterness,
and hatred.

Finally, I choked out the words, "If I forgive, I'm afraid they'll
get away with everything they did to me."

I wasn't ready to forgive that day.

As I continued to walk with Jesus, He showed me that the things
done to Him seemed unforgivable, yet while hanging on the cross,
He cried out for the forgiveness of those who put Him there.

I learned that when we forgive, we actually free ourselves.

Every day that I held onto what people did to me, I carried the
weight of hurt, anger, bitterness, and resentment. It dripped off of
me, affecting every area of my life. Many precious moments were
wasted being angry at someone who wasn't even there. I failed to
enjoy some of the happiest moments of my life, because I was too
busy being angry about something that happened years before.

15

When I chose to forgive, over time, the bitterness and anger disappeared. I found I was able to enjoy my todays—to *really* enjoy them. I was free.

You can be free of the weight of unforgiveness, bitterness, and anger. You don't have to carry them anymore. You can be free to enjoy your todays without the pain of years gone by getting in the way.

Don't let those weights steal one more moment of happiness. Choose to forgive.

PRAYER

Lord, I choose to forgive _____ for _____. I release this person into your hands. I give you all my hurt, resentment, bitterness, and anger toward them. I don't want to hold onto it anymore. Set me free from every weight that holds me to them. In Jesus' name, amen.

DAY 9

A Key to Daily Strength

Unto thee, O my strength, will I sing: for God is my defense,
and the God of my mercy.
—Psalm 59:17 KJV

Something was missing.

I felt empty. My strength was gone, and I was filled with a longing for what I had once had.

"What happened, Lord?" I asked.

A few days later, I was reminded about the importance of making time for worship. I realized that as life had grown more hectic, I had let my time with the Lord slowly slip away.

The next day, I dropped off my kids at school, came home, and spent some time worshipping the Lord. As this became a regular habit, my strength increased, and I felt the presence of the Lord permeate every part of my life.

Time spent with God in prayer and worship touches every other part of your life. It brings peace when you walk through storms and gives you an inner strength you wouldn't otherwise have.

You can sing to the Lord while you're getting ready in the morning, while you're in your car, cleaning house, or even when you're taking a walk.

Let a song rise within your spirit and sing to the Lord today. Feel the act of worshipping lift you to a higher place, helping you rise above the storms of life. As you worship, you will receive

17

encouragement and hope from your heavenly Father. He will give you the strength you need to walk through one more day.

Worship the Lord today. Dip into the well of His presence and find refreshment for your soul.

PRAYER

Lord, I choose to worship you today. Fill my life with your presence and give me hope where I have been hopeless and courage where discouragement has come. Touch the broken places in my heart with your love and help me rise above the storms of life. In Jesus' name, amen.

Peace in the Middle of the Storm

Peace I leave with you, my peace I give unto you: not as the
world giveth, give I unto you. Let not your heart be troubled,
neither let it be afraid.

—John 14:27 KJV

I couldn't stop what was coming, and it was continually on my
mind.

My stomach was tight, my jaw clenched.

I sat talking with a friend about it one day. She listened to me
vent my frustrations and fears then looked me in the eye and said,
"What does God say about that?"

Her words stopped me cold.

I hadn't been paying attention to what God said about this. I
had only been rehearsing the circumstances in my mind over and
over again, stressing myself out.

I went home and asked the Lord for forgiveness and asked
Him to show me what *He* said about this. I soon found a verse that
covered the entire situation. And the next morning, I repeated that
verse out loud over and over while I was getting dressed for the day.

I did it the next day and the next.

After a week of repeating that Scripture while getting dressed,
the fear I had about the situation was gone. Circumstances hadn't
changed, but I had refocused my attention to God's Word.

The event came and went.

19

Instead of what I had feared, I saw God's hand in the situation. By focusing my attention on God's Word instead of on the circumstances, I gained a measure of peace. I have done this several times now with different circumstances and the results are always the same: the longer I focus on the answer—God's Word—instead of on the problem, the more peace I have.

When circumstances have you stressed out, fearful, or discouraged, ask the Lord to help you find a Scripture that covers the situation. Keep your mind on this Scripture, speaking it out loud to yourself sometime during the day. Commit the Scripture to memory and think on it while you have a quiet moment. You will find that peace overtakes stress, fear, and discouragement.

PRAYER

Lord, I release the battle to you, and I declare that this battle is yours and not mine. Forgive me for not trusting you. Help me to focus my attention on your Word instead of on the circumstances around me. In Jesus' name, amen.

DAY 11

One More Day

O thou afflicted, tossed with tempest, and not comforted,
behold, I will lay thy stones with fair colours, and lay thy
foundations with sapphires.

—Isaiah 54:11 KJV

Tears streamed down my face, and I fell to my knees in front
of my husband.

I hung my head for a moment then looked back up at him.

"All I have done is serve Him." I said through my tears.

The eyes I looked into mirrored my own pain.

We had served the Lord with our whole hearts, given Him all
we had, yet our world was falling apart around us. How could one
family endure such chaos in the course of just a few months?

We had come to a point of decision.

Would we continue to serve the Lord? Or would we give up
and quit?

What if we gave up when what God had promised us was just
about to happen? What if we gave up just before the breakthrough
came?

That day, I was exhausted, discouraged, fearful, and full of
self-pity. I felt I couldn't walk through one more day. But I had to
decide. Would I choose to trust, or would I give up?

Jesus will help me get through one more day.

God did what He said. He helped me through one more day, and every day after that. Although there were more tears, He helped us through all of it. We saw His hand move, showing us He was there in every situation, every heartache, and every pain. He didn't always take it away, but He helped us walk through it.

When the battle is fierce, when you are weary and feel you can't go on anymore, when giving up seems so tempting, I implore you not to give in. God is on the move even when you can't see it yet.

Sit before the Lord and draw strength from His presence.

Jesus will help you through one more day.

PRAYER

Lord, I release every battle, every challenge, and every hurt and pain to you. I choose not to give up but to rely on your strength. Encourage me and give me what I need today. Refresh my weary soul. In Jesus' name, amen.

DAY 12

He Thinks You're Beautiful

He restoreth my soul; he leadeth me in the paths of righteousness for his name's sake.

—Psalm 23:3 KJV

I love to walk through antique stores and museums. Each piece I look at has a story.

I find myself asking, who owned this a hundred years ago? What was life like for them?

Some pieces are shrouded in mystery, and you can only guess at who owned them. Others come with a short paragraph or two of who they belonged to. When I look at antiques, I see stories, stories of people long since gone, possibly with only this antique left to tell their story.

What did they struggle with? What were their joys and sorrows? What made their heart ache? What made them happy? Did they end up with the love of their life, or did they die lonely and bitter?

Some pieces are so beaten up and worn out that it seems no one would ever want them. They are passed up every day for other pieces that seem more beautiful. But there is a right person for everything.

Some come to the antique stores to find just those very pieces that no one else would want. They are able to look past the dents, dirt, and grime to see the true value of the piece. They know that with just a little work, or sometimes a lot, they can restore this piece, making people who previously would have passed it up, stop and admire its beauty.

God has created in each one of us something beautiful and unique, a gift for the world around us. You may have been passed by or rejected by others. But God will never reject you when you come to Him. He sees the beauty in you and has a plan for your restoration. You are worth more than you will ever know. Invite the Lord in to do a work in your heart and in your life, you will not be disappointed.

PRAYER

Lord, I invite you into my heart to begin the restoration process. Help me to know that you love me, to be secure in your love, and to understand how very valuable I am to you and to your kingdom. Thank you that you have plans for my life and a plan for my restoration. I surrender my own plans to you and agree with your plans for my life. In Jesus' name, amen.

DAY 13

Keep It from Slipping Away

Give ear, O people, to my law: incline your ears to the words
of my mouth.
—Psalm 78:1 KJV

Sometimes, without even realizing it, we can let relationships slip away.

We know we should take time, but there are so many other things on our plates.

My husband and I realized we needed to start dating again when we felt life getting busy. Kids, appointments, jobs, school—we needed to *make* time for each other. When we began dating again, our relationship grew stronger. We grew closer, and the Lord started to do a work in our relationship.

Today we have a strong marriage because we have taken the time to build our relationship with one another.

It works the same way in a relationship with God. We can either let it slip away without us noticing, or we can be intentional and make time to be with Him. Read His Word to find out what He says and have a conversation with Him about it. As we do this more and more, we get to know our heavenly Father, our relationship with Him becomes stronger, and we ourselves grow more mature and spiritually strong.

Be intentional. Don't let your relationship with God slip away. Take some time today and spend it with the Lord.

PRAYER

Lord help me to be intentional about a relationship with you. Teach me your ways and remind me to seek you first in every situation. In Jesus' name, amen.

DAY 14

Making It a Habit

Thy word is a lamp unto my feet, and light unto my path.
—Psalm 119:105 KJV

I lifted the old journal from the chest and felt it crinkle in my hands. Opening it to the very first page, I found that it was one of my attempts to start reading the Bible and journaling every day. Empty pages told the story of how my goal had not been accomplished.

How I wished I would have done what I set out to do!

I blamed my children, my messy house, and my busy schedule. The truth was, it was my choice.

I came to a place where I made a quality decision that I would spend time in the Word of God every day. As I started practicing my new habit and growing in the Lord, I began to notice if I missed a day. I found myself to be grumpy and emotional without time in the Word.

I realized being in the Word was a habit that made me stronger in every area of life. I was growing, and other people were noticing the changes in me too.

Reading the Word will not only help you become spiritually strong, it will affect every area of your life. It will speak to your heart, give you comfort, and it will encourage you not to give up when you feel discouraged.

The Lord's Word is a treasure of wisdom, comfort, and guidance. Open your Bible today and ask the Lord to speak to your heart.

PRAYER

Lord Jesus, I choose to be in your Word today. Give me understanding by your Spirit. Help me to put your Word into practice in my life. Comfort and heal my heart, encourage me where I need to be encouraged, and give me wisdom for today. In Jesus' name, amen.

DAY 15

A Dangerous Root

Looking diligently lest any man fail of the grace of God; lest
any root of bitterness springing up trouble you, and thereby
many be defiled
—Hebrews 12:15 KJV

The atmosphere was sweet in the women's church meeting as
we all shared things God had been doing in each of us. But
that was about to change.

A woman stood up next to her table. Anger and bitterness
spewed from her lips as she grumbled about her life. The atmosphere of the whole room changed.

There was a high probability that this meeting could turn from
focusing on God's goodness to grumbling about our own problems.

This reminded me of the Israelites.

The Israelites were God's chosen people. Yet in the desert, they
complained, grumbled, and gave voice to their bitterness. Instead
of inheriting the Promised Land, they stayed in the wilderness,
settling for way less than what God had planned. They never saw
the good plans of the Lord come to pass in their lives and died in
the wilderness (Num. 14).

Bitterness can spread like a virus. One person gets it and the
next thing you know, two others are agreeing with them, speaking
out more grumbling and bitterness. It's like a nasty weed that

29

springs up in a beautiful garden, choking the life out of what's been planted there.

We all have a choice. We can choose to get rid of bitterness by forgiving, or we can choose to let it grow, feeding it by complaining, grumbling, and dwelling on the wrongs done to us.

Forgiveness may seem hard. But when you make a choice to forgive and continue to forgive every time the situation comes to mind, it is possible. You can walk free from the snare of bitterness and unforgiveness. They don't have to be a part of your life anymore.

What will you choose?

PRAYER

Lord Jesus, I want to choose forgiveness. I don't want to stay in bitterness and unforgiveness any longer. I give you what was done to me and all the hurts of my heart. I release those who wounded me into your hands and pray you would give them what they need. Help me to walk in forgiveness and not let any bitter root spring up in me. In Jesus' name, amen.

DAY 16

Realize His Love for You

That Christ may dwell in your hearts by faith; that ye, being
rooted and grounded in love
—Ephesians 3:17 KJV

I was finally getting it.
  Memorizing Scripture about God's love was helping me realize
God loved *me*. For years I believed the lie that no one loved me,
and I struggled with the sting of rejection.

Each time I declared the truth of God's love, the lie that I wasn't
loved or wanted was getting weaker. To confirm I was growing
stronger, one morning during church, my friend turned to me and
said, "You seem stronger somehow."

I wish I would have continued memorizing Scripture's on God's
love, but I stopped and started again. Life was busy, distractions
came. But eventually, memorizing and declaring Scripture became
a way of life.

Today, I can feel it when I don't get Scripture into my heart.
When I'm not declaring the Word of God, I feel weak. When I am
memorizing and declaring Scripture over myself, strength rises
in my spirit. I am comforted by God's Word, encouraged, and
reminded of the love of my heavenly Father.

Find a Scripture that speaks to your heart about God's love for
you. Declare that Scripture out loud throughout your day.

31

You may not notice it right away but as you continue, you will find yourself stronger and more secure in God's love for you. You will become rooted and grounded in God's love.

PRAYER

Heavenly Father, I pray that I would be rooted and grounded in your love. Give me an unshakable faith in the knowledge of the depth of your love for me. In the name of Jesus, I break the power of the lies that have said I am not loved. I command those lies to leave me now, in Jesus' name. I declare that I am loved by my heavenly Father.

DAY 17

Your Healing Is Coming

> Now unto him that is able to do exceeding abundantly above
> all that we ask or think, according to the power that worketh
> in us.
> —Ephesians 3:20 KJV

It was a constant battle.

I knew I was broken; the hurt was ever with me. And I so wanted to be healed.

Unresolved hurts are an open door for the enemy to come and cause torment. And torment is what I was in. I felt alone, like I was in constant pain, and no one could see it. I was expected to function like anyone else, and when the hurt and pain *did* show itself, it was obvious that most people wanted to run. They didn't know how to help me, and I felt even more alone.

In the midst of spiritual anguish and brokenness, I gave my tears to God. Some days that was all I could bring. The battle raged on. And I kept crying out to God for healing.

Some days I was hopeful, and other days I wondered if my life would ever be different.

Slowly, day by day, the Lord worked in my heart. He picked up each broken piece individually and did a healing work in me. He did not just glue my heart back together where the broken pieces all showed. Like the master artist that He is, He took that brokenness and created something beautiful in me.

When you have been in the battle a long time wondering if things will ever get better, when you are weary, worn out, and feel you have prayed all that you can pray, sit quietly before the Lord. Receive His love and encouragement to go on another day.

Don't give up.

Your healing is coming.

God has heard your prayers.

And His answer is more than you could ask or imagine.

PRAYER

Father God, I pray that you would give me what I need today. I give you my broken heart and pray that you would pick up the pieces and put me back together again, better than before. Thank you that you hear my prayer and that you have a plan for my restoration. In Jesus' name, amen.

DAY 18

Strength to Hold On

Don't be afraid," he said, "for you are very precious to God.
Peace! Be encouraged! Be strong!"
—Daniel 10:19 NLT

My family was shaken to the core.

My mother, who I had seen just days before, had suffered a massive stroke.

The family waited together while she was in surgery. Some were quiet, some talkative. The sun shone in from outside, gracing the hospital room with its light. The world outside seemed to go on as normal, while inside, we waited.

Thoughts of the last time I saw my mom swam through my mind. It was only for a few moments as I ran an errand near her house. I looked back at her while walking away, "We should go to lunch sometime."

She smiled, "I would really like that."

During this time of trauma, I found strength from moments already spent with the Lord in prayer and in His Word. What I had taken time to put into my heart and mind came out in a time of family crisis, giving me strength and comfort, helping me to hold on to my faith.

You may not know what tomorrow will bring. But you can draw strength for tomorrow by spending time with the Lord in the Word and prayer today.

Take some time today to put the Word of God into your heart and mind. It will give you strength for tomorrow.

PRAYER

Father God, help me to put your Word into my heart on a daily basis. Let me draw strength from your Word today so that your Holy Spirit may comfort me throughout my tomorrows. In Jesus' name, amen.

DAY 19

You Are Not Hopeless

If we confess our sins, he is faithful and just to forgive us our
sins, and to cleanse us from all unrighteousness.
—1 John 1:9 KJV

I wasn't paying attention.

Lost in thought while driving down the freeway, I missed my
exit. I had to find another route that would get me to my college
class in time. The whole way I berated myself for daydreaming and
missing the way I was supposed to go.

While stopping at a red light, I heard the Lord in my spirit so
clearly, "If you ever go down a wrong road, I'll make sure you get
back on the right one."

We've all taken a wrong step at times and found ourselves on
the wrong path, some of us hopelessly lost. It is in these times that
we can cry out the name of Jesus. He answers our heart's cry, takes
our hand, and leads us the right way once again.

Never run away from God when you've made a mistake. Never
think He doesn't want you anymore. He loves you, mistakes and
all, and He will help you get back on the right path.

You are not a lost cause.

You are not too far gone.

You are not forgotten.

Cry out to the Lord, and He will help you. He loves you and
has been waiting for you to cry out to Him.

You are loved. You are precious. You haven't made too many mistakes. He has not rejected you. You don't have to be good enough for God; He takes you just as you are.

It's when you come close to the Lord that your life is changed, not when you are far away from Him, trying to clean yourself up.

Jesus is not afraid or even offended by your brokenness. He is more than willing to pick you up, take your hand, and lead you home.

You are a child of God: precious, treasured, and important to Him. Come home. He loves you so very much, and He's waiting for you.

PRAYER

Lord, I give you my whole self. I give you all the wrong roads I've taken and every mistake I've made. I come to you with no pretense just as I am Lord. I am broken, hurting, and I've made mistakes. Thank you that you accept me just as I am. You are not offended by me coming to you in my brokenness, but you are compassionate and merciful. I give you my life and ask that you would make the wrong things right and do a beautiful work in me. In Jesus' name, amen.

DAY 20

Grumbling Costs

Rejoice always, pray without ceasing, in everything give
thanks; for this is the will of God in Christ Jesus for you.
—1 Thessalonians 5:16–18

I was acting like the Israelites.

My husband took me out to breakfast, and all I did was
grumble.

I grumbled about what was happening in our lives. I grumbled
because we were still waiting for things we'd prayed for. I grumbled
about the way people treated me. I grumbled about the food.

My husband sat across from me, eating his breakfast in silence.

Do you really think this is what he wants to talk about?

The thought hit me like a ton of bricks. Gratefulness had left
the building, and I needed to invite it back in.

I thought of the Israelites, and how their grumbling cost them
the good things God had planned for them (Num. 14).

I, too, was waiting for things God had promised me. And I,
too, was grumbling.

When I find myself grumbling now, I know I need to stop. I
need to give those complaints to the Lord and ask Him to remind
me to be thankful instead. I've noticed that when I turn my focus
from grumbling to thankfulness, my whole outlook changes.

Grumbling is a habit that can be overcome. When you feel like
grumbling about one thing, find two things to be thankful for.

You will find that life is much brighter when you take the time to be thankful.

Do you struggle with grumbling? Spend five to ten minutes thanking the Lord for things He's done for you already and for the promises He's given you. Then take your prayers to God and ask Him to work in the situation you were tempted to grumble about.

PRAYER

Father God, thank you that you love me so much you sent Jesus to die on the cross for me. Thank you that I have breath in my lungs. I pray that you would work in me a heart of gratefulness. In Jesus' name, amen.

DAY 21

He Hears Your Cry

So do not worry, saying, "What shall we eat?" or "What shall
we drink?" or "What shall we wear?"
—Matthew 6:31 NIV

"Lord, I don't have enough money for baby formula." It was a
simple prayer, but I would soon see that God had heard.

I took my son in for his monthly checkup. At the end of the
visit, the nurse asked what kind of formula he used. She gave me
a sample and with a thank you, I headed out the door.

But then, she called me back. I turned to see a pile of formula
in her arms. "These are going to expire."

She kept handing me more and more formula, until my diaper
bag was so full it wouldn't hold anymore. I left the doctor's office
thanking and praising God that He had heard my prayer and for
providing my baby with food.

When you say the simplest of prayers, God hears you.

You are His precious child, and He is listening.

Keep in remembrance the answers to even your smallest
prayers, so when a need arises, you will be able to say with
confidence, God has heard my prayer before, and He hears it now.
My God is faithful.

41

PRAYER

Father God, you are faithful, and you hear my prayers. Help me not to be anxious or worried about anything but to trust in your care for me. Create in me an unshakable trust in you. In Jesus' name, amen.

Making a Choice

In you, Lord my God, I put my trust.
—Psalm 25:1 NIV

"She wants to know if you would like her daughter's old sled." My dad brought me the news.

Excitement gripped me. I could see myself sledding down our hill in the snow, the wind blowing through my hair and the envy of all my friends. I imagined who would want to ride with me and how much fun we would have.

No longer would I have to watch from the sidelines, begging for a ride from someone else. I would have my very own.

The day finally came. I was supposed to pick up that sled and take it home.

The woman who said she'd give it to me had it in her hand. The red rails gleamed beneath the dirt caked upon them but with a little elbow grease, they would shine like new.

But then, the woman looked at it longingly. "I can't. I'm sorry, I just can't."

And with that, I no longer had a sled.

I tried to swallow my disappointment, took in a deep breath, and watched the woman walk away with what I'd been promised.

The same story kept threading its way throughout my life, and I learned not to trust. I became weary of getting my hopes up, weary of the disheartening let down when people didn't keep their word.

So when it came to trusting God, it was hard for me to believe what He said was true. I didn't want to get my hopes up anymore.

I told God about my struggle. I knew He wanted me to trust Him, but I was afraid. Finally, one day I declared out loud, "Lord, I choose to trust you with this."

The more I chose to trust Him, the more I saw Him work in situations as only He could. The more I chose to trust by choice, the more I saw Him keep His word.

You, like me, may have learned that you can't trust people's word. Experience may have taught you not to trust, that the only person you can depend on is yourself.

By choice, choose to trust the Lord. Declare out loud that you trust Him, no matter what your feelings may be telling you. Continue to declare your trust in Him and watch your heavenly Father go to work in your life.

PRAYER

Lord, I choose to trust you. I pray that you would heal the places in my heart where I have learned not to trust anyone. Give me the strength to trust you and your Word. In Jesus' name, amen.

DAY 23

Finding Comfort and Strength

Consider it pure joy, my brothers and sisters, whenever you
face trials of many kinds, because you know that the testing
of your faith produces perseverance. Let perseverance finish
its work so that you may be mature and complete, not lacking
anything.

—James 1:2–4 NIV

I thought they'd be safe people. They said they were Christians.
In my ignorance, I shared things I should have kept between
me and God. At the time I was immature and knew nothing of
comparing the fruit in people's lives with what they said about
themselves.

Instead of finding the love and support I hoped for, I became
a target of the very people I thought I could trust.

I called an older woman who was like a mentor to me and told
her what happened.

"Some people see through the lenses of their past experience. It
may not have anything to do with you but with what they haven't
dealt with in their own lives." Her wise words gave me comfort.

We talked a little more, and before we hung up, she said, "I
want you to go turn on some worship music and worship for a
while. Then, I want you to go get your Bible and read it out loud."

As I followed her directions and worshipped the Lord, I could
feel the hurt and pain slipping away, and when I opened the Word,

I was met with comfort and encouragement. No longer was I down and depressed. I was still a little hurt, but it wasn't overwhelming anymore.

When we go to God with our hurt and pain, He will comfort us and give us strength to walk through one more day. The situation we are walking through may not change right away, but God will strengthen us through the time we spend with Him in worship and the Word.

Turn on some worship music today and then read the Word aloud. You will find strength and comfort in the Lord.

PRAYER

Father God, I lift up to you the sorrow, pain, and brokenness that have plagued my heart. I ask that you would take it from me as I worship you. Fill me with your strength, your joy, and make me whole again. In Jesus' name, amen.

DAY 24

How Do I Get Joy?

Do not sorrow, for the joy of the Lord is your strength.
—Nehemiah 8:10

I was among friends but having such a hard time.
We met before church to pray for the service. But this day I needed prayer for myself. After the meeting, I shared what I was going through.

In a moment I was surrounded by prayer warriors, all declaring and praying God's truth over me.

One man said, "Carolyn, the joy of the Lord is your strength." How could that be?

I wasn't joyful; I was depressed most of the time and fraught with fear.

How could the joy of the Lord be my strength when I didn't have any?

The Lord is so good at answering our heartfelt questions. I wanted to learn how to have the joy of the Lord, because I truly didn't know how. It didn't anger the Lord or even phase Him that I asked that. It only moved Him to show me the truth.

Over time, I learned the joy of the Lord comes when we put our focus on Him and Him alone.

It comes when we worship even in the midst of trying circumstances. It comes when we focus on God's truth instead of

47

what's going on around us. We don't hide our heads in the sand but declare God's truth in the midst of life's storms.

When depression, despair, or discouragement try to steal your joy, say to them, "I do not receive you, and I tell you to go in Jesus' name."

Then, declare God's truth over your situation. If you don't know what God says about what you're going through, ask Him to show you. He may even point you toward someone who has been through something similar.

Be in the Word, prayer, and worship on a consistent basis.

Daily declare out loud, "The joy of the Lord is my strength."

PRAYER

Lord Jesus, I pray that your joy would overtake my life. When the storms of life come, let me be in perfect peace, because my mind is stayed on you and your word (Isa. 26:3). I bind all distracting and hindering spirits off of my mind now and break your power in Jesus' name. I declare that I have the mind of Christ (1 Cor. 2:16). Thank you, Jesus, for your peace. In Jesus' name, amen.

DAY 25

It's Time to Break the Chains

Then Peter came to him and said, "Lord, how often shall my brother sin against me, and I forgive him? Up to seven times?" Jesus said to him, "I do not say to you, up to seven times, but up to seventy times seven."
—Matthew 18:21–22

Recently, one of my children repeated what an adult in our extended family said to another adult at a family gathering. It wasn't good, and I was sad my child heard the bitter words. We had a conversation about forgiveness and why it is so important.

It got me to thinking about my own struggle with bitterness, anger, and unforgiveness.

I can never go back and change what happened to me. It happened.

Being angry did not fix it.

Being bitter did not take away the pain but only made it worse.

The pain, like quicksand, sucked me in; it was all I thought about. Because I had run away from dealing with the pain and instead held on to the offense, I was chained to the past, unable to walk free.

It was only when I made the choice to forgive, lifting the painful thoughts and memories up to Jesus, that the Lord started to wipe the pain and bitterness away.

Being angry and bitter about what happened to you will only keep you chained to the past, unable to move forward, unable to heal.

It's time to break the chains.

God has so much more for you.

It's time to move on.

Choose to forgive and when you see the person who hurt you or memories of the past come up, choose to forgive again.

Bind Satan.

I have had to say to him, "Satan, I bind you from tormenting me with those painful memories anymore. I command you to stop now, in Jesus' name."

Daily lift the pain up to the Lord. A prayer I have prayed is: "Lord, I release this pain and brokenness to you, and I ask you to heal my heart in Jesus' name."

You cannot change what happened to you. But you can invite Jesus into your pain, and by His presence and power, He can bring healing to every broken place in your heart.

Cry out to Him. You are worth saving. You are worth healing.

PRAYER

Lord, I give you the brokenness. I give you the pain. I choose to forgive _____ for _____. I choose your ways Lord and invite you into my brokenness. Free me from the chains of the past. Free me from all bitterness, anger, and unforgiveness. Come into my heart and set me free. Thank you that you are my deliverer, that you have heard my prayer, and you will be faithful to answer it. In Jesus' name, amen.

DAY 26

Look Up

Why, my soul, are you downcast? Why so disturbed within
me? Put your hope in God, for I will yet praise him, my Savior
and my God.
—Psalm 43:5 NIV

"I know the cure for depression," our teacher said one morning.
I enjoyed every minute of the counseling class at Bible
college. Our teacher was in her eighties; she was funny but also
taught from the heart.

"If you want to stop being depressed, find fifty things to be
thankful for," she announced.

I didn't know it at the time, but I was heading straight into
a traumatic season. Crisis after crisis, one after another, hit our
family hard. We wondered where God was at times and how these
things could happen.

Yet, my teacher's voice played over in my mind, "Find something
to be thankful for."

In the heart of continual trauma and storms, there were days
I couldn't remember what I was supposed to do next, let alone
think clearly. But when I purposely chose to turn my focus from
the storms raging around me to God's faithfulness, I felt different
physically. My mood lifted and peace came. I knew God was there
even if I couldn't see Him.

You are not alone in the storms of life. Instead of letting them steal your peace and drag you into a pit of depression and despair, choose to be thankful for *something*.

One of the most powerful things you can do when the world seems to be falling apart around you is lift your hands toward heaven and give thanks.

PRAYER

Lord, thank you that you love me so much you sent Jesus to die on the cross for me. Work in me a heart of gratefulness. I ask that your Holy Spirit would remind me of things to be thankful for. Help me turn my focus from the negative onto the good that you are doing in the midst of the storms. Hold my hand through this Lord and lift me from the pit of depression. In Jesus' name, amen.

DAY 27

You Are Loved

For the Father Himself loves you, because you have loved Me,
and have believed that I came forth from God.
—John 16:27

The pastor speaking that day had a daughter who was only a
few months old.

He told of the prayers he prayed for her every night: prayers
that she would not reach out to people to meet her needs but would
fully know the love of her heavenly Father.

I was glad this man prayed over his daughter yet also saddened
for myself. Sometimes we can be happy for people and sad for
ourselves all at the same time, asking the Lord, "Why didn't I get
that?"

Like that pastor prayed for *his* daughter, our heavenly Father
wants us to know His love and in fact, has Jesus interceding for us
right now (Rom. 8:34).

He wants us to know that even in trials and pain, He is with us
and brings us through it. We never walk alone (Ps. 139). He wants
to turn the curses in our lives into blessings (Deut. 23:5) and heal
us of the things that have hurt and wounded us (Ps. 147:3).

We have a heavenly Father who loves us and isn't afraid of any
emotional pain we may struggle with. He is never too busy and
never tires of listening (Ps. 121:4). In fact, He can't wait to spend
time with you.

Your heavenly Father loves you more than you can ever imagine. His love is so much greater than any earthly father's love could ever be. Even if no one on this earth has ever shown you the love of a father, you can pray what that pastor prayed for yourself.

Pray that you would fully know the love of your heavenly Father.

PRAYER

Lord, show me the wonders of your great love. I pray I would know your love so deeply that I wouldn't go to others to meet my needs but my relationship with you would exceed all others. And Lord, where others on this earth have failed me, where I've been hurt, wounded, and bruised, I ask that you would heal the broken pieces and make me whole again. In Jesus' name, amen.

DAY 28

From Broken to Beautiful

My beloved spoke and said to me, "Arise, my darling, my
beautiful one, come with me."
—Song of Songs 2:10 NIV

The camping trip was a special one.
After having some friends to our campsite for dinner, my
husband and I lay on a blanket outside and gazed up at the stars.
The sky was clear and every star bright. With the exception of
rustling as an animal passed by, the quiet of the forest surrounded
us. Darkness turned black, making the stars shine even brighter.

We drank it in for as long as we possibly could.

Such beauty. Such peace.

In His wisdom, God created each one of those stars and just
as each star is set in its established place, so He created you with
love in His heart and a beautiful plan for your life.

He gazes upon you as we gazed upon those stars. The beauty
of your love for Him pleases Him, and He cannot look away (Ps.
139). He thought of you before the foundation of the world (Eph.
1:4), sent Jesus to die for you so you could have eternal life, and
has an established place for you—a plan for your life that only
you can fulfill.

Nothing that's happened can take away that plan. He is a master
artist and only works those things into the fabric of His design for
your life. Those things you think are too painful, too ugly to even

look at or mention—it is those things, when given to Him, that He weaves in to His plan with care. He picks up the broken pieces and turns the dirt and grime of our pasts into breathtaking beauty.

You don't have to stay in your pain and hurt any longer. Give Him your tears, anger, and shame. Allow Him to come in to the hidden places of your heart to begin the process of healing.

He is a master artist with a plan for your restoration, and it's a beautiful plan.

PRAYER

Lord Jesus, I give you my broken heart, my hurts, my anger, my shame. You are not afraid of my brokenness but want to pick up every piece and turn it into something beautiful. Thank you that you will never stop loving me and nothing can steal your plans for me. I say yes to your plans Lord. In Jesus' name, amen.

DAY 29

Paid in Full

Therefore, if anyone is in Christ, he is a new creation; old
things have passed away; behold, all things have become new.
—2 Corinthians 5:17

I didn't want those brushstrokes in the painting of my life anymore.
I couldn't forget them. Each day I was reminded of the
mistakes I had made and wished I had a big eraser to wipe it from
my memory and everyone else's too.

Certain people were sure to take every opportunity to remind
me of a past I'd rather forget. It seemed they took pleasure in heap-
ing shame upon my head even years after I turned my life around.

I knew God had forgiven me, yet I couldn't seem to rise above
the mistakes of my past.

Until one day, I had a conversation with a woman who asked
me a direct question. "You've forgiven other people, but have you
forgiven yourself?"

The minute she asked it, I knew I had not. I'd been beating
myself up and letting others beat me up too for mistakes I'd made
years ago, carrying a burden Jesus already paid for.

Forgive yourself for the mistakes you've made. Jesus already
paid the price. You don't have to walk in condemnation anymore.
If you've asked God for forgiveness, He has already forgiven you
and wants you to move on.

Stop carrying the burden of your past with you every day. It's weighing you down, not letting you move forward. Cut ties with it by forgiving yourself and forgiving others.

Jesus wants you to be free.

PRAYER

Lord, I ask forgiveness for _____. I receive your forgiveness, and I now choose to forgive myself. I will no longer walk in condemnation. I thank you, Jesus, that you bore this on the cross for me, and I am free. In Jesus' name, amen.

DAY 30

Hold on to Your Dream

We have different gifts, according to the grace given to each of us.
—Romans 12:6 NIV

As a child, I spent many a day playing outside, only to think of a story and run *inside* to write it.

When I was eleven, my friend came to my house and found me up in a tree reading a book. She wanted me to come and play. I proceeded to tell her I couldn't possibly come down from that tree, because I was reading the best book in the world. If I remember right, it was a Nancy Drew book.

She shook her head as she walked away.

My friend did not understand my love of writing and books. Sometimes *I* didn't even understand why I loved them so much. I only knew I did.

As I grew older, teachers encouraged me in writing, saying I had a gift.

You also have a gift. God has given you a talent, a love for something that maybe other people don't quite understand.

At a Christmas Eve service last year, a picture came to me of what the world would look like if we all gave up on our dreams. Everyone in the church held a lit candle, and the lights in the church were turned down. Each person's candle shone brightly, and it was a beautiful sight.

59

When we collectively blew our candles out, the sanctuary was dark, and it was hard to see. At that moment, the Lord spoke to my heart, and I realized that if I listened to the naysayers or gave in to discouragement, my corner of the world would be a dark place. I would be missing out on the unique light God has given me to shine.

Don't give up on the dreams God has put into your heart, for He himself has put them there. He has given you a unique light to shine in this world, and someone needs that light.

Decide you will not give up, and ask the Lord what your next step is.

PRAYER

Lord Jesus, your Word says that the gifts and callings of God are irrevocable (Rom. 11:29). So I pray, Lord, that you would stir up your gifts within me. I want to be a shining light for you in this world. Thank you that you created me with a special purpose in mind. In Jesus' name, amen.

Never Too Broken

I will say to the prisoners, "Come out in freedom," and to
those in darkness, "Come into the light." They will be my
sheep, grazing in green pastures and on hills that were previously bare.

—Isaiah 49:9 NLT

I believed the lie that I was too broken for God.

I didn't understand how He could reach through my brokenness and bring me into joy and peace.

I had been torn down so much, I was afraid to think anything
good about myself lest that be taken away too. I cried at the drop of
a hat. I told my sad story to anyone who would listen. I was unable
to move forward, tormented by a past that would not let me go.

The people I ran to ran away from me, not wanting to hear
another word of my pain. Rejection wrapped itself around my heart,
and I felt even more alone.

It seemed nobody understood, and the only one who truly knew
what I went through was God. I knew I could run to Him, and He
would not run away.

I learned that He was the best one to go to with my pain. I was
never rejected and never alone. As I spent more and more time
sitting at His feet, He lifted me out of torment, breaking the ties
that held me to my past.

You are not too broken for God. He is not running away from you but has a plan for your restoration. Bring it all to Him and set it at His feet.

Come to Him with your tears; He'll wipe each one away.

Come to Him with your burdens; He'll carry them for you.

Come to Him with the things that torment you; He will break the chains off of your life.

He will carry you out of the darkness, set you on your feet, and help you live again. He will give you a life of joy and heal your broken heart.

Stick with Him day after day and enter into the process of letting Him restore your life.

You are not too broken for God. He will not leave you here. You are so precious to Him, and He loves you.

PRAYER

Lord Jesus, thank you that I am not too broken for you. I can come to you any time of day or night, letting it all out to you, and you are there to listen to my cries. Thank you that I am never alone, but you are with me in the midst of my pain, and you have a plan for my restoration. I give you permission, Lord, to come and restore my soul. In Jesus' name, amen.

Speak Life

Death and life are in the power of the tongue
—Proverbs 18:21 KJV

"Who of you are encouraged to go out and do great things when people speak negative words over you?"

No one raised their hands.

Our Bible college teacher had made his point, words are powerful.

The saying, "Sticks and stones will break my bones, but words will never hurt me" is an out-and-out lie. Words cut deep into the core of your soul. They can tear the fabric of your heart and leave it broken for a lifetime.

You do not have to be the victim of the ugly words spoken over you anymore.

When negative, hurtful words come to mind, you can pray and break their power: "In the name of Jesus, I break the power of ungodly words spoken over me, and I forgive the person that spoke them. I remove the arrows from my heart and mind right now, and I command those words to fall to the ground and have no more power over me. In Jesus' mighty name."

Do this each time negative words come to mind to break their power and forgive the person who spoke them.

Then, replace those negative words with the truth of God's Word. Memorize Scripture about what God says about you, letting it go deep into your heart by speaking it over yourself.

Negative words cut deep, sometimes to our very core. But there is a weapon against them, and it is the Word and power of our Lord Jesus Christ. Break the power of negative words and replace them with God's truth. As you enter into this process, you will soon find yourself walking free. One day you will notice those negative words no longer have power over you.

PRAYER

Lord, I choose to forgive those who have spoken ugly, hurtful, and condemning words over my life. I break the power of those words in Jesus' name. Lord, I invite you into my heart and ask you to heal every broken and hurting place. I pray that the poison of those words would be removed from my heart. I ask, Father, that you would help me to replace those negative words with the truth of your Word. I want to walk free. In Jesus' name, amen.

DAY 33

Receive His Plan

Your ears shall hear a word behind you, saying, "This is the
way, walk in it," Whenever you turn to the right hand or
whenever you turn to the left.

—Isaiah 30:21

I knew exactly where I was going and what I wanted to do.
And I was on my way.

I was finally going back to school to become a librarian.

Until one day, in prayer, the Lord brought up Bible college.
A part of me deep down had once longed to go to Bible college,
but I had given that up. I didn't believe that I, of all people, could
actually do that.

So, at first, I ignored God.

But He kept bringing it up.

Then people started talking about Bible college in conversation.
I hadn't told anyone what God had brought to my mind, yet it was
beginning to be a regular topic.

I finally said to the Lord, "If you *really* want me to go to Bible
college, show me where to go."

Days later a few miles from home, I turned my head at just the
right moment to see a sign that said, *Seattle Bible College.* I had
no idea it was there. Come to find out, it's the same college my
husband's family had gone to.

Over and over God confirmed His word to me, showing me the next step He wanted me to take. He had called me to do something I didn't think I could ever do.

When I said yes to His plan, it was through His strength that I walked into it. And through His strength, I walked the platform on graduation day, holding a diploma in my hands.

God has a plan for your life too. His plans are better than any plan you could make for yourself. He has created you to fit like a puzzle piece right into His plan for you.

You may not feel like you can do what He's called you to do. Take a step forward, relying on Him, and He will show you that through His strength, you can do all that He's asked of you.

You are not alone in His plans for you. He's with you every step of the way. Only take the next step, and He will meet you there.

PRAYER

Lord, I thank you that you have a very special, unique plan for me. I receive your plans and surrender my own plans to you. Show me the next step I should take and lead me in the way I should go. In Jesus' name, amen.

DAY 34

Seek His Face

Seek the Lord and His strength; seek His face forevermore!
—Psalm 105:4

Healing didn't come overnight.
It took years.

I saw God's goodness in each little step I took toward Him, and slowly He put my life and heart back together again.

It began with worship and prayer, counseling, Bible college, and then He led me to a ministry where people who were trained in deliverance helped me to heal. My husband and I felt the call to enter into training ourselves, and that is where my life was changed forever.

Each of us had to deal with our own stuff before we helped anyone else and in training to help others, I myself received a miraculous healing. The wounds of the past were cleaned out, and the enemy's hold on me was broken. He had no more legal right to my life.

God has a plan for your healing. Each step you take toward Him is an important one. The time you spend with Him, giving Him your tears and forgiving those who have hurt you, is time that you are giving the Lord permission to work in your life.

Don't dismiss the time you spend with God as unimportant or let it be eaten up by other things that need to get done. It is His presence that leads you to a place of healing.

He is the Lord who heals you (Ex. 15:26).
Seek His presence daily. It will change your life forever.

PRAYER

Lord, I pray that you would give me the courage to seek your face every single day of my life. While I am happy and joyful, when I am broken, and when I am not, let seeking your presence be a most important part of my life. In Jesus' name, amen.

DAY 35

Rise Above

But those who wait on the Lord shall renew their strength;
they shall mount up with wings like eagles, they shall run and
not be weary, they shall walk and not faint.

—Isaiah 40:31

L ife seemed like one big storm to me.
　　While I walked with the Lord through my healing, He spoke
to me about being like the eagle. When storms come, other birds
take cover but not the eagle.

The eagle rises above the storm, soaring over it, sailing on the
wind, letting the storm carry it to a higher place.

You, too, can find a higher place when the storms come. Instead
of focusing on the storm, seek refreshment through worship and
prayer, letting the storm carry you right into your heavenly Father's
presence.

In the middle of the storm, it may be hard to see that it will
ever end. Keep pressing on. Do not quit! You will see the end of
this storm; God will not leave you here.

Let the storms of life take you to a higher place in the presence
of the Lord. He will carry you through each one and though the
storm may be raging, you will be at peace in His presence.

Lift your eyes off of the storm and on to Jesus, letting Him carry
you to a higher place of knowing Him, trusting Him, and relying
on Him. Just watch as He works in every area of your life.

PRAYER

Lord, I ask that you would help me know that I am never alone in any storm of life, that you will never leave me nor forsake me. Create in me a deep trust in you, knowing that nothing can snatch me out of your hand. In Jesus' name, amen.

DAY 36

Fear Not

I sought the Lord, and He heard me, and delivered me from all
my fears.

—Psalm 34:4

Fear gripped my very life. It directed every move I made.
Years after childhood trauma, I lay in bed, my heart pounding, afraid to even close my eyes. I held my body rigid, waiting for whatever it was I was afraid of to appear. This happened to me most nights, and I could hardly sleep. There came a point where I was afraid to even leave my house. I would walk outside and fear would grip me so forcefully I hurried back inside.

It was only Jesus who helped me overcome that. I still struggle with fear sometimes, but it's not debilitating anymore. I walk out of my house without fear. I lay down at night, and my heart does not pound. When fear comes, I speak to it. I say, "God has not given me a spirit of fear, but of power, love, and of a sound mind (2 Tim. 1:7). In Jesus' name, fear, leave me now! I will not let you hold me back anymore."

If you are struggling with debilitating fear, know that Jesus will not leave you here. It may take some time, but you can overcome fear, leave it behind, and be free from its captivating grip.

Each day, walk with Jesus and ask Him to deliver you, quoting Scriptures about freedom from fear. It will have to remove its hold on you. Follow God's leading and guidance and let Him direct you into your freedom. If you need to seek medical help, then seek it, and don't let anyone make you feel guilty about it.

God is not mad at you for being afraid. He understands what you went through, but He also doesn't want you to stay trapped by fear. Ask Him to deliver you from every fear and create in you a heart full of trust in Him.

PRAYER

Heavenly Father, I ask your forgiveness for letting my life be directed by fear. I thank you, Lord, that you are my deliverer and that you want me free from the grip of fear. Deliver me from every fear and give me a security in you. In Jesus' name, amen.

Give Him the Pain

For the Lord will comfort Zion, He will comfort all her waste places; He will make her wilderness like Eden, and her desert like the garden of the Lord; joy and gladness will be found in it, thanksgiving and the voice of melody.

—Isaiah 51:3

Some people have pain everyone can see.
And then there are others who suffer in silence. The pain they experience can go on for years: mental torment, fear, worry, nightmares. Every day they live in heartbreak and anguish.

I know what it feels like to suffer alone, unable to run away from the pain, wishing you could just be OK, seeing counselor after counselor, trying to deal with things that never seem to go away. After a while, you start to wonder if you will ever find freedom.

I have been there. I have felt all of these things.

I have felt the sting of rejection from people who are supposed to be able to help. I have felt alone, suffering in silence because no one wanted to hear it anymore. I have felt hopeless, alone, and afraid.

I questioned whether I would ever get better.

And then, Jesus.

He was not afraid of my pain. He did not run the other way when I came to Him. He did not reject me and decide He couldn't help after all. In fact, He knew exactly what to do.

You are not too far gone. You are not alone. You no longer need to suffer in silence. There is someone who will never tire of hearing your story or wiping away your tears. He never sleeps, so you can call on Him any time, day or night. He does not want you to run away from the pain, but instead, give it to Him, He is able to bear it. He is gentle and will help you walk through it, leading you into freedom.

You do not need to stay in your pain anymore.

Today, I want you to give Jesus your pain. Hold out your hands and imagine you are holding every hurt, wound, and bruise, everything that has caused you anguish of soul. Now lift it up to Him, turn your hands over, and shake them out. Drop that pain you are holding into God's hands.

It's time to let the restoration begin.

PRAYER

Lord, I don't want this pain, anguish, and mental torment anymore. I release it to you, Father. I pray that you would heal my heart, heal my mind, and rid me of this pain. Help me to see that there is hope for me in you to walk out of this pain and into the joy of the Lord. Jesus, make yourself real to me. Help me to find comfort in you. In Jesus' name, amen.

DAY 38

Shake It Out

Cast your cares on the Lord and he will sustain you; he will
never let the righteous be shaken.
—Psalm 55:22 NIV

The pastor wiped the burdens from my shoulders.
But they were still there.

I didn't understand that he was praying they *would* be wiped
away, that he sensed God wanted to take them from me. I had to
give those burdens over to the Lord and stop hanging on to them
as if I myself could somehow make them better.

I went through a season where I would give my burdens to the
Lord, but then, because I didn't fully trust Him, I took them back.
When I realized I'd taken them back, I had to try and give them
over one more time.

Later on, the Lord put someone in my life who would help me
give those burdens to Him for good. This man was a mentor and
spiritual father to both my husband and me.

One day we were all talking, and I told him how I tried and
tried to give things over to the Lord but kept taking them back,
even when I didn't consciously want to. It was such a struggle for
me; I wondered if I'd ever be able to fully let go.

"Hold out your hands," he instructed.

When I did, he said, "Lift those burdens up to the Lord."

As I lifted my hands, still holding those burdens, he reached out and turned my hands over, so my palms faced downward. "Now shake it out. Shake those burdens out of your hands. Declare to God, they are your burden now and not mine."

When I declared these things and physically shook the burden out, I could feel something happening. Physically letting the burdens go was helping me to emotionally and mentally let them go.

I finally understood why that pastor had wiped the burdens from my shoulders physically. I needed a physical action to go with a spiritual decision.

I started to do this every time the thought of a burden came up. I kept giving those burdens to God over and over until I had truly let them go.

What burdens have you been carrying?

You were not meant to carry those burdens on your own. They are weighing you down. Every time a burden tries to lay itself on you, lift it up to God, turn your hands over, and shake it out. Tell God you give it to Him; it's His burden now and not yours.

As you let go, God will take those burdens. They won't be yours anymore.

You will walk free.

PRAYER

Father God, I give you each and every burden that I'm carrying today. I declare they are not my burden anymore, but they are yours. I don't want them anymore, and I give them to you. I let go and declare this is your battle and not mine. In Jesus' name, amen.

DAY 39

A Picture of Forgiveness

For if you forgive men their trespasses, your heavenly father
will also forgive you.
—Matthew 6:14

"Would you forgive the debt?"
The person who asked me this question owed
thousands of dollars.

Everything in me wanted, needed, them to pay me. Yet when
they asked the question, something moved deep within my spirit.

I didn't answer them right away. I asked for time to think about
it. And after praying and talking with my husband, I felt I was
supposed to forgive this debt.

As far as I was concerned, they didn't owe me the money
anymore. There was no way they could pay it back.

As I went through the process of forgiving this monetary debt,
I was struck with the understanding that this is a picture of what
God has done for us. In the sins of our past, we racked up quite a
debt. But when we come to the Lord and ask Him to forgive our
debt of sin, He wipes the slate clean through the blood of Jesus
(1 John 1:9). We don't owe that debt anymore. It's been forgiven.

And then God showed me this is also what it looks like to forgive
others for the wrongs they have done to us. When someone wrongs
us in any way, whether it be a small slight or something that has
cost us great pain and loss, we want them to pay.

We, in a sense, have charged them with the debt of the wrong they have done to us.

That person, whether they are sorry or not, cannot give us back what was stolen. They can't give us back the dignity that was taken. They can't make up for the heartache, sorrow, and grief they caused.

They can *never* give it back.

They cannot pay the debt.

We can spend our lives in bitter disappointment, trying to get something back from that person we've deemed should pay, or we can choose to forgive, and trust God to make it up to us.

It doesn't mean they get away with it. It doesn't mean what they did was OK. It means you are not going to try and collect that debt anymore. You understand they cannot pay it back to you.

If you choose to forgive, you will be able to heal from the wounds that were inflicted, and you can ask God to make it right—to give you a double blessing for each of your troubles (Zech. 9:12).

PRAYER

Lord, I choose to forgive _____ for _____.
I realize that _____ can never repay me for what was done. _____ can never give me back what was stolen.
I break spiritual ties with _____ right now. I release all the anger, hatred, bitterness, and resentment I feel toward _____, and I ask, Father, that you would heal my heart.
I ask for a double blessing for each of my troubles. In Jesus' name, amen.

DAY 40

Strength to Keep Going

But David strengthened himself in the Lord his God.
—1 Samuel 30:6

He was gone for just a little while.

And while he was gone, they burned his house down. Not only that, his family was kidnapped. His friends' families were taken and their houses burned too. No one knew if they would ever see their loved ones again.

Looking at the destruction and loss around them, they were overcome with grief and wept till they could weep no more.

His friends decided it was his fault, for it was he who convinced them to go. He heard a few whispers of how they wanted to kill him, and he silently slipped away.

He sat down, feeling completely and utterly alone: his family gone and his friends wanting him to pay with his life. His heart was broken so badly he could physically feel it. Weariness came over him and while he was alone where no one could see him, his body shook with sobs.

Though he felt like sinking into despair, instead David reminded himself of what the Lord had already done and asked Him for strength and direction. The Lord guided him in getting his family back (1 Sam. 30).

All was restored.

In the midst of battle, the enemy would like to throw you off kilter. He would like to have you blame and question God. He would like nothing better than to stop the progress you've already made and keep you from moving forward.

When things fall apart, how do you find strength to keep standing? How do you not fall down into the depths of despair, wondering why this happened and where was God when it did?

Take time to be with the Lord and listen. Be in prayer consistently. Read the Word of God daily. It is through His Word that God gives encouragement, direction, and wisdom. Seek refreshment and strength through times of worship. Remember what the Lord has already done for you and remind yourself that He will not leave you here.

Do not lose heart.

God has taken you this far, and He's not about to abandon you. He has a plan for your restoration.

PRAYER

Jesus, I need you now. I need your encouragement, your comfort, and your healing touch. As I open my Bible today, speak directly to my heart. As I spend time in worship and prayer, give me comfort and direction. Show me the way out of sorrow and despair. In Jesus' name, amen.

DAY 41

Rest in the Battle

But you will not even need to fight. Take your positions; then
stand still and watch the LORD's victory. He is with you, O
people of Judah and Jerusalem. Do not be afraid or discouraged. Go out against them tomorrow, for the LORD is with you!"
—2 Chronicles 20:17 NLT

My stomach was tight. My jaw clenched.
A situation our family was dealing with had gone on far
too long. It had looked like things were getting better, but then
came a turn for the worse. Our hearts were broken, and we were
dreadfully afraid for someone we loved.

In the midst of all this, my husband and I were scheduled to
serve at a church retreat. I was ready to cancel; I didn't want to serve
anyone else. And I was also a little bit mad at God. How could He
let this happen when we served Him so faithfully?

My husband took some time to get away by himself, and the
Lord ministered to his heart.

He called me and said, "We're supposed to go to this retreat.
We're supposed to go *because* of what we're going through."

I didn't understand it, but I knew in my heart he was right.

With battered hearts and weariness in our soul, we set out to
the retreat, telling God we didn't have anything to give, and He
was going to have to do it all.

While we were in corporate prayer before the retreat even started, I heard the Lord speak to my heart; "Carolyn, I will fight your battles for you. When you try and fight your own battles, I can't fight them."

I realized I needed to take my hands off and just trust Him.

When you feel the battle is fierce and you're tired and worn out, could it be possible that you are trying to fight the battle yourself?

Decide now that you are going to rest in the Lord. Take your hands off the situation and declare the battle is His. Tell Him you refuse to fight it yourself anymore.

Declare this every single day until you see the victory.

PRAYER

Father God, I release this battle to you. It is your battle and not mine, and I refuse to fight it on my own. I give it into your hands, and I choose to trust that you will fight the battle for me while I rest in you. Thank you, Father, that this battle shall not take me down, but I shall walk in victory. In Jesus' name, amen.

DAY 42

A Beautiful Mess

He has made everything beautiful in its time.
—Ecclesiastes 3:11 NIV

My husband loved the house.
I wasn't quite sure about it.

We stepped onto the porch; half of it was missing.

I came through the front door, wondering if I dared to go inside. My husband walked in with great confidence. What met us was a beautiful staircase, the original architecture from the 1920s.

I was struck with its beauty, standing regally among the mess. But then my eyes moved toward the floor, covered in dirt, dust, and debris. I took in the holes and cracks in the walls and the stains that looked like they had replicated themselves throughout the house. When we moved toward the kitchen, we found that there wasn't even one there.

I stood in the middle of that mess, waiting to leave. But my husband was in love and talked of all the things he could do to make the house beautiful again.

While I pondered why my husband loved this house so much, the Lord brought a thought to my mind: "Weren't you once broken too?"

When other people looked my way and saw only brokenness, the Lord saw someone valuable, beautiful, and loved. He saw not

83

what was but what could be. He saw the plans He had for me and the beauty He would work in me as I surrendered my life to Him.

Each one of us has a broken place inside of us. Some may be more broken than others, but it is the Lord's work in us that makes us beautiful. The more broken we are, the more beautiful His work becomes. As we allow Him entrance into our lives, He restores, rebuilds, and makes things that were once unlovely, more beautiful than you could ever imagine.

You may have been overlooked, passed by, judged, and forgotten. Rejection may have climbed its way into your heart, and you may feel unloved and alone.

But the Lord looks upon you with love in His eyes. He sees beauty and value in you.

Give Him your mess, and He will make it into something beautiful.

PRAYER

Father God, I thank you that you have not forgotten me. I invite you in to work in my heart, making each broken piece into something beautiful. I choose not to let others define me anymore but to let you define me. I am beautiful, valuable, and loved by you. I am cherished and treasured, and you look on me with love in your eyes. Help me to see myself as you see me. In Jesus' name, amen.

DAY 43

A Quality Decision

Establish Your word to Your servant, who is devoted to
fearing You.
—Psalm 119:38

I was trying to read my Bible.

Yet when I did, it's as if something covered my mind so I could not understand it. I put it down. Then, days later, I would pick it up, try again, and put it down.

After many stops and starts, I grew frustrated. I wanted to grow in my faith, and I had heard that being in the Word is what would help me grow.

I asked for prayer from a trusted friend and made a quality decision to make a daily habit of being in the Word, whether I got something out of it or not.

I was *going* to be in the Word every day.

Things began to change. I started to understand it, and I also better understood the sermons I heard. I grew spiritually, and a great hunger was birthed in me. I had to be in the Word; I needed it like I need breakfast every morning.

I later learned that the enemy of our souls doesn't mind if we say we're Christians and do nothing else. But he hates it when we pray, and he especially hates it when we start getting into the Word. He will try to distract us as we read, telling us such things as: we don't have enough time, there's no point, or we couldn't possibly understand it.

Decide to be in the Word on a regular basis. Pray before you read, asking the Lord to show you what He wants you to see. Read it aloud, letting it change the atmosphere around you. As you get the Word deep into your heart by reading it daily, it will do a work in you.

PRAYER

In the name of Jesus, I put on my helmet of salvation, my breastplate of righteousness, my belt of truth, and my shoes of the gospel of peace. I take up my sword of the spirit and my shield of faith (Eph. 6). I declare that I have a sound mind and command all lies of the enemy to fall away. I have the mind of Christ (1 Cor. 2:16). I plead the blood of Jesus over my heart and mind, over my home, and over my family. Jesus, today I make a quality decision to be in your Word. I pray that you would help me to become strong in you by reading, studying, and retaining the Word of God. In Jesus' name, amen.

DAY 44

Victory over Negative Thoughts

I will call upon the Lord, who is worthy to be praised; so shall
I be saved from my enemies.
—Psalm 18:3

The battle lasted all day.

Negative thoughts assaulted my mind ruthlessly. I didn't know how to stop them, and so I dwelt upon them for hours. Because of this, my emotions rolled up and down like a yo-yo.

Later I learned that's exactly what the enemy wanted. He wanted to steal my peace, steal my joy, and rob me of the blessings of the day (John 10:10).

My negative thinking patterns did not change overnight. Sometimes I still have to deal with them. But I have learned that when negative thoughts come, I do not have to let them steal my peace and joy.

When your mind is assaulted by negative thoughts, there is a weapon available to you. This weapon will bring you back to a place of believing the Lord. It is the weapon of praise.

Every time a negative thought comes, praise the Lord out loud. Praise Him for His promises to you and that His word is true. Rebuke the negative thoughts and declare God's truth over your mind.

You can have victory over negative thoughts. Take back your peace of mind by praising the Lord out loud.

PRAYER

Lord, I thank you that you have given me the weapon of praise. In the name of Jesus, I break the power of all ungodly assignments over my mind. I cast off fear, anxiety, and worry right now. I do not receive negative thoughts anymore. Lord Jesus, I give you every tormenting, negative thought, and I ask for your healing touch upon my mind and heart. In the name of Jesus, I break the arrows of the enemy off of my mind right now and declare that I have the mind of Christ. In Jesus' name, amen.

DAY 45

Giving Him Expectations

And they that know thy name will put their trust in thee: for
thou, Lord, hast not forsaken them that seek thee.
—Psalm 9:10 KJV

This person failed me in a big way.

Yet I kept hoping. I kept letting myself be around them
because I truly hoped that someday they would change. Someday
they would love me the way they were supposed to. Someday they
would be different.

But each time I opened myself up to them, once again I found
myself hurt and wounded. I so wanted them to be what I'd hoped
they would be, that I let them wound me over and over again.

After being wounded too many times, I started learning about
boundaries and letting myself grieve what this person would never
be, letting go and facing what really was. Every day, I lifted the pain
of what they hadn't been to me up to God and asked for His healing.

One day when I saw them, I realized I wasn't expecting things
from them anymore. I looked at them and knew they would never
fulfill the needs they were supposed to have met.

And I was OK because I learned I have a heavenly Father who
cares for me and is able to fill every void like no one else can.

God will never fail you. He understands the wounds of your
heart, and He knows what you've been through, understanding

89

like no one else ever could. He knows exactly what you need and wants to heal your heart.

Ask the Lord to help you let go of expectations that you may have placed on others, lifting the pain of what you hoped they would be up to Him. Let yourself grieve those relationships. Don't be afraid to face the pain, for in facing it, you will find God's comfort and healing.

Every day, lift those relationships up to Him, releasing all expectations you had into His hands. And thank Him for His healing. Thank Him that He is your heavenly Father and that He will never fail you.

Choose to trust in your heavenly Father, and let Him in to heal your heart.

PRAYER

Lord, I give you the expectations that I may have put on other people. I forgive those who have failed me, and I release them into your hands. I pray that you would heal my heart of the brokenness and wounds caused by people who didn't love me as they should have. Help me to see and know the depth of your love for me and to walk every day in that love. In Jesus' name, amen.

DAY 46

Mind Protection

For the weapons of our warfare are not carnal but mighty in
God for pulling down strongholds, casting down arguments and
every high thing that exalts itself against the knowledge of God,
bringing every thought into captivity to the obedience of Christ
—2 Corinthians 10:4–5

When I am doing something I don't need to think through, such as taking a shower or driving, sometimes my mind will start to wander.

Because of the environment I grew up in, usually it wanders to the negative. I used to let myself dwell on these thoughts but no more. I discovered that I have a choice in what I think on.

When negative thoughts come, I stop them in their tracks by speaking Scripture out loud. If it's something I'm afraid of, I thank God that He has not given me a spirit of fear (2 Tim. 1:7). If it's something that reminds me of my past, I thank God that I am a new creation (2 Cor. 5:17). And if it's something someone else did, I remind myself out loud that I have forgiven them and release them once again into God's hands.

If the thoughts are of bad memories, I tell Satan in Jesus' name that he will not torment me with these memories. I ask Jesus to heal the memories so that when I do remember them, it won't hurt anymore. I lift the memories up to God and release them to Him;

they are not my burden anymore, but His. I have placed them into His hands.

Finally, I thank God out loud that He will give me a double blessing for each of my troubles (Zech. 9:12).

A negative thought can be like an ugly worm crawling into our minds. But when we have the Word of God written on our hearts, it is much less likely that a negative thought can make its way in, causing us unneeded distress.

You don't have to be the victim of negative thoughts. You have a choice on what you think on. Start putting the Word of God in your mind and heart on a daily basis, and soon those negative thoughts will be kept at bay, unable to do their dirty work.

PRAYER

Lord, I pray for your protection over my mind. In Jesus' name: I speak to every ungodly assignment over my mind, I cast you down and cut you off, I declare that you are unable to do your works of darkness any longer. I declare that I have the mind of Christ. Lord Jesus, help me to fill my mind with your Word, little by little, day by day, till it overflows within me. In Jesus' name, amen.

DAY 47

Your Weapon

And take the helmet of salvation, and the sword of the Spirit,
which is the word of God:
—Ephesians 6:17 KJV

I was so nervous walking into that class. I had never even touched a gun, let alone shoot one.

The first thing we learned was gun safety. Never point the gun at anything you don't want to shoot. Keep your finger off the trigger until you're ready to fire.

Finally, it was time to go to the range. I held that gun in my hand, prepared to fire. My heart pounded wildly, and my insides shook with fear, but I held that gun steady.

Gently, I moved my finger onto the trigger.

Bang!

That day, I faced my fears and learned how to properly use a gun. The instructor said I should come into the range several times a week to practice, or else I would forget what I learned. Only through regular practice would shooting become second nature to me.

It is the same way with the Word of God. Paul calls the Word of God the sword of the Spirit (Eph. 6:17).

If you are in the midst of battle and have not practiced by putting the Word into your heart and mind, you could easily be shot down by the deception and schemes of the enemy.

The Word is your weapon. Practice using it every day. If you do, you will find that when the battle rages, you are prepared, practiced, and able to wield your sword of the Spirit.

Wielding that sword, you will walk into the victory God has prepared for you.

PRAYER

Heavenly Father, as I read your Word today, speak to my heart. Help me to become proficient at using the sword of the Spirit and most of all, Lord, help me to live out the truths you show me. I invite you into my heart to do a mighty work through your Spirit and your Word. In Jesus' name, amen.

DAY 48

A Picture of the Father

Behold what manner of love the Father has bestowed on us,
that we should be called children of God!

—1 John 3:1

The question still lingered in my mind.

I tiptoed downstairs in the quiet of the morning while the rest of my family slept. The question heavy on my heart; I sat quietly before the Lord, reflecting on the day before.

We had served at the Cleansing Stream retreat and saw God do some amazing things in the hearts of His people. Yet in my heart, I still missed our spiritual father. He had mentored and trained my husband and me for the retreats, and this was the first time we had served without him. At the beginning of the year, he had to move out of state suddenly, and we missed him terribly.

And so, the question lingered: Why would God give me a spiritual father and take him away after only one year?

I sat in the stillness of the morning, happy and sad all at the same time. That's when I heard it. The still, small voice rising up within my spirit.

"I have been your God, but I would really like to be your Father."

Tears slid down my face. I had known in my head that God was my Father, but I had never truly known it in my heart.

From that moment on, I understood that the Lord put this man into our lives to give us an example of what He Himself wanted to be.

If you have ever felt that you didn't know what a father's love looks like, for whatever reason at all, know that the Lord wants to show you a picture of His love.

He has been your God, but He would really like to be your Father.

PRAYER

Heavenly Father, I pray that you would give me a picture of what a father's love looks like. I receive you as my Father, Lord, and not just as my God. And I thank you that you receive me as your precious child: beautiful, valuable, and dearly loved. In Jesus' name, amen.

DAY 49

Breaking the Power of the Past

The Spirit of the Lord GOD is upon Me, because the LORD has anointed Me to preach good tidings to the poor; He has sent Me to heal the brokenhearted, to proclaim liberty to the captives, and the opening of the prison to those who are bound.
—Isaiah 61:1

As a young lady, I decided I wanted to leave the past behind and start a new life. Little did I know that the past I ran away from came with me, carried deep within my heart. I couldn't run away from it.

I ended up in a situation that was very much like the one I'd tried to leave behind. By His grace and mercy, God picked me up out of that mess and gave me a new life, one that only He could give.

When you are hurting, wounded, and bruised, often you are drawn to people who are also hurting. Without even meaning to, you reenact the past all over again. Old patterns think they can dictate our lives, because they have not been interrupted.

It's time to interrupt those old patterns and learn something else.

Get into God's presence through worship and prayer. Start spending time daily in God's Word. Don't just read through it quickly but read it slowly, letting it speak to your heart.

Memorize Scriptures on how much God loves you and who He says you are. In doing this, the lies you've been told about yourself will be broken.

Ask the Lord to break the unhealthy patterns in your life and to give you new, healthy patterns. When we invite Him in, He responds. It may not be instantaneous, but He will go to work in your life.

You can be free from unhealthy patterns of the past; they don't have to hold you captive anymore.

PRAYER

Lord, I pray that you would deliver me from repeating the patterns of my past generations. Send people into my life who will show me examples of healthy patterns and who will help me to grow in you. Thank you that you have come to set the captives free and that my past does not define my future. In Jesus' name, amen.

DAY 50

Permission to Feel

A time to weep, and a time to laugh; a time to mourn, and a
time to dance;
—Ecclesiastes 3:4

Memories clung to my mind, unwilling to let go. They tormented me and the more I tried *not* to think about them, the more pressing they became.

Things would happen in everyday life that reminded me of a traumatic event. In an instant I was taken back, overwhelmed with fear, and tormented by emotions that held me captive with no plans to release me.

For many years, I tried to pretend I was OK. I wore a permanent smile to hide the pain. And when the anguish rose up within me, I swallowed it down, never giving myself permission to feel.

Yet those feelings manifested themselves in different ways. I was frequently sick, easily offended, and overreacted to ordinary situations. I pretended all was well, trying to ignore the turmoil and pain, but I wasn't fooling anyone.

It's OK not to be OK. The Lord never expected you to try and hold it all together yourself. Your feelings are very real, and there is nothing wrong with you for feeling them.

In the Old Testament, people wept, cried out, tore their clothes, and sat in ashes as a significant way of showing their grief (Gen. 37:34).

It's OK to feel your feelings; you don't have to keep them hidden anymore.

When you read the Psalms of David, often you will see him crying out to the Lord, letting his feelings out. Afterwards, he proclaims the goodness of God and his trust in Him.

It's OK to be angry. It's OK to be hurt, and it's OK to weep.

It's OK to feel your feelings.

PRAYER

Father God, I don't want to keep the heartache and anguish bottled up anymore. I want to feel my feelings and be free of them. I pray that you would show me healthy ways to release these feelings and put safe people in my life to help me to do so. I invite you in to help me feel every feeling I have held in. I release these feelings to you. I choose to trust you as you walk me through my grief and into healing. In Jesus' name, amen.

DAY 51

He Knows Your Pain

The LORD is close to the brokenhearted; he rescues those
whose spirits are crushed.
—Psalm 34:18 NLT

Many a day I walked, head down with tears in my eyes, away from people who misunderstood me, defined me by my pain, and treated me as If I had something they didn't want to catch. At times all I wanted was to crawl into a hole and hide away for the rest of my life.

Behind closed doors, I would let myself cry, hiding the pain of their rejection from the world. And in the midst of that hurt and pain—pain so desperate and deep that it caused me to fall to the floor and shake with sobs, wondering if I'd ever be happy or even be normal—I heard the still, small voice of the Lord rising up within my spirit.

"I love you. I love you, and I understand what you are going through. I understand what happened to you, I saw what no one else saw, and I will take care of you."

"Sit here with me a while and share your heart with me. I want to hear all about it. I will never run away. I am not afraid, and I will never reject you."

Your heavenly Father sees your pain.

He understands.

He knows.

And He wants to heal you.

Come as His child, sit on your papa God's lap and tell Him all about it. He wants to hear your voice, is waiting to hear your heart's cry, and can bring healing to your heart.

Come to the one who truly loves you and can heal your heart of every hurt, wound, bruise, and pain. He will not reject you. He is not afraid of your pain and will never abandon you.

PRAYER

Father God, I choose to come to you now. Give me the courage to trust you and pour out my heart to you. I ask, Father, that as I do, you would bring healing to my heart. Let me find peace in your presence. In Jesus' name, amen.

DAY 52

Strength through Praise

The Lord is my strength and my shield; my heart trusted in
Him, and I am helped; therefore my heart greatly rejoices, and
with my song I will praise Him.

—Psalm 28:7

During Bible college, chapel was one of the most precious times
for me.

We heard speakers who inspired us to keep going even through
trials and pain. This day was no different. We were greatly encouraged, and then the speaker opened up a time of prayer.

The person who prayed for me spoke of things in my life only
someone who truly knew me would know. He went on, "Some have
hit bumps in the road and have quit because of them, but she has
encountered craters. She will not quit but will go the whole twelve
rounds. She will not quit!"

He was right in what he prayed. I had encountered craters, big
ones. At times things had gotten so bad I could feel myself falling
into despair, self-pity, and depression. There were days I had to
force myself to even get out of bed in the morning.

Some days I hadn't even wanted to go to my classes. But I knew
in my heart that God had told me to do this, and I was going to
follow through.

I would finish.

When things were dark, something that helped me tremendously was entering into the presence of God through worship and praise. When I spent time worshiping the Lord, I was lifted out of the clutches of despair even for a little while. I can tell you with confidence that worshiping the Lord in song changed my life.

If you have struggled, as I did even to get out of bed in the morning, start some worship music first thing. Sing to the Lord throughout your day. Take some time for just you and the Lord, entering into His presence through worship and praise. It will lift you out of despair and depression, bring you to a higher place, and help you carry on one more day.

PRAYER

Lord, I thank you that you have given me the gift of worship and that I can enter into your presence through thanksgiving and praise (Ps. 100:4). As I worship you today, I invite you in to heal my heart. Give me the strength I need for today and fill me with joy in your presence. In Jesus' name, amen.

DAY 53

A Peaceful Place

My people will live in peaceful dwelling places, in secure
homes, in undisturbed places of rest.
—Isaiah 32:18 NIV

Even as a teenager, I longed for the peace of God.
Down the hill from our little house was a church. And on
that church property was a picnic table. I would walk down to
that church and sit at that picnic table for hours, enjoying the
atmosphere of peace in that place.

As I grew to know my Lord and Savior, I recognized that peace
is found in His presence. And when I invited His presence into my
home, the atmosphere changed to a place of peace.

You, too, can create an atmosphere of peace in your home. It
can be a place where you and other people find rest.

Make your home a place where you worship the Lord in song.
Sing praise to the Lord as you are getting ready in the morning,
doing dishes, or other housework.

Read the Word of God out loud in your house and on your
property. You'll be surprised at how doing these things on a
consistent basis will change the atmosphere of your home.

Get some anointing oil and pray through your home, anointing
doorways and entrances. Declare that this is a place of peace and
invite the Holy Spirit to dwell in your home. Always pray in Jesus'

name, because in His name is where we have our authority (John 14:13).

You can have a peaceful dwelling place that is free from fear, darkness, and despair. Invite the Lord into your home today so it can be a place of rest for you and for others.

PRAYER

Lord, I invite you into my home, and I ask that you would make it your dwelling place. Let your peace rest here, Lord. I welcome your presence into my home. In Jesus' name, amen.

DAY 54

Changing Your Mind

And do not be conformed to this world, but be transformed by
the renewing of your mind, that you may prove what is that
good and acceptable and perfect will of God.
—Romans 12:2

The teacher of our Bible class spoke of her struggle when she
first received salvation. Thoughts kept coming to her mind
that she wasn't really saved at all.

She took a Scripture that applied to the situation and wrote
that Scripture on a card. She kept that card with her and looked at
it multiple times a day.

After a few months, the lie was gone. She didn't believe it
anymore.

Her story inspired me.

I had always struggled with feeling unloved. So after hearing
her story, I decided I would try this too.

I wrote down a Scripture about being loved by God. And like
her, I looked at it and spoke it out loud several times a day.

After a few weeks, I noticed I was changing. I wasn't so quiet
anymore, and I was feeling more secure. When people behaved
unkindly, it didn't have the effect on me as it had before.

And this was only in a matter of weeks.

I imagined what doing this for my whole life could do!

Paul tells us in Romans 12 to renew our minds with the Word of God. When I first heard the phrase, *renew your mind*, I wanted to do it but didn't know how.

Now I understood that renewing your mind meant replacing the lies of the enemy with God's truth by putting His Word into your mind on a daily basis.

What we believe about ourselves affects the way we act. When we change those beliefs, the Lord can do great things in and through us.

What thoughts are you struggling with?

Meditate on the truth of God's Word, looking at it and speaking it out loud several times a day.

Doing this could change your life.

PRAYER

Father, I pray that you would give me the endurance and the will to keep my mind on your Word. Keep me from getting distracted. I break the enemy's hold on my mind right now and declare that I have the mind of Christ. In Jesus' name, amen.

DAY 55

God Has Not Forgotten You

Can a woman forget her nursing child, and not have compassion on the son of her womb? Surely they may forget, yet I will not forget you.

—Isaiah 49:15

It's hard to enjoy today when you carry the pain of many yesterdays with you.

For years, things that happened in everyday life reminded me of trauma and abuse from the past. A simple word or action, even a smell, had me reliving an event I would rather forget. Nightmares plagued me. I hardly slept, and fear tormented me day and night.

When you've been through traumatic situations, it can be hard to let go of the hurt and pain, and it can be hard to move on. You may have tried to let go, yet the pain seems to hold you captive, unwilling to release you from its grip.

This happened to me. I forgave and forgave, but the feelings never truly went away.

One day while a group of people surrounded me in prayer about this very situation, someone asked, "Do you need to forgive them?"

"I have forgiven, over and over, but something is still there. It just won't go away." Tears came to my eyes. I so wanted to be free.

That's when one woman came and sat in front of me. She put her hands on my shoulders and said, "What do you want to say to them?"

And then it all just came flowing out. The feelings of hatred, anger, abandonment, and bitterness all came out into the open.

After I had let those words carry the feelings out of me, the people who prayed with me walked me through the process of forgiving one more time. This time, it was for real.

I walked out of that ministry time free: free of the hatred I had held in my heart for so long and free of the burden of what had been done to me. My todays have become my own. I am no longer tormented and haunted by a past I can never change.

You may have been hurt terribly and tried to forgive, only to be tormented still. You may have wondered why it hasn't worked for you and if you would ever truly be free.

Could it be possible that there are still things you need to say to the person who hurt you? You may not be able to say it to them directly, and it might not be safe to do so. But, you can seek out trusted people to help you get your feelings out.

You can be free. God has not forgotten you. He has the perfect plan for your restoration, and He knows exactly what you need.

PRAYER

Lord, thank you that you have a plan for my healing, that you have not forgotten me and you know exactly what I need. Lead me and guide me into what you have for me. I want to forgive. I want to be free. In Jesus' name, amen.

DAY 56

Healing Time

Restore unto me the joy of thy salvation; and uphold me with
thy free spirit.
—Psalm 51:12 KJV

Every step you take with Christ is a step closer to your healing.
When I started making worship a part of my daily life, my
mind was taken off of my pain and put onto God. A little time in
the morning had a major impact on the rest of my day.

Every time I came to the Lord in worship and prayer, He, in
His mercy, picked up another piece of my broken heart and began
the process of putting it back together again.

And then, He led me into a life-changing healing.

For the longest time, my voice had been so soft no one could
hear me. I rarely spoke at all, and when I did, it was barely a whisper.
I had learned to hide in all areas of life, knowing that if no one saw
or heard me, I couldn't become their target. I became invisible.

This life-changing experience happened during a time of
ministry in which a few trusted people gathered around just to
pray for me. During this prayer time, the subject of my voice was
brought up, and lies that I had been told about myself came out
into the open. With the help of the people who prayed with me,
I broke the power of those lies through Jesus' name and the part
of myself I had hidden away for so long came out of the darkness
and into the light.

When you seek the Lord in worship, you are entering into His presence, and in His presence, healing comes. You are not a lost cause. You don't have to hide anymore. Your Father, Papa God, longs to hear your voice and to see you walk into freedom. Come into agreement with His plan for your healing and watch Him go to work.

Today, take another step toward Christ by spending some time with Him in worship.

PRAYER

Lord, I invite you into my heart, my mind, and my life. I come into agreement with your plan for my restoration, and I thank you that each time I spend time with you in your presence, you are doing a work in me. No time with you is ever wasted time. In Jesus' name, amen.

DAY 57

Facing the Pain

But now, this is what the Lord says, he who created you,
Jacob, he who formed you, Israel: "Do not fear, for I have
redeemed you; I have summoned you by name; you are mine.
When you pass through the waters, I will be with you; and
when you pass through the rivers, they will not sweep over you.
—Isaiah 43:1–2 NIV

Darkness surrounded me.
    My heart beat double time, and I felt as if it would jump
out of my chest. *What was that noise?*

My husband slept peacefully beside me, but I, bound by fear,
lay with the weight of terror upon me. I was afraid of the night. As
a child, nighttime is when bad things happened.

I wanted to forget the past, leave it behind, and never think
of it again. Yet here I lay, terrified at nothing in the middle of the
night. The past would not leave me alone.

In the days and months that followed, the Lord impressed upon
me that the only way I would be free from the past was to face it. I
had tried to run away from it for so long, and it had never worked.

I was afraid to face the pain, afraid to touch the hurt hidden
deep within me, afraid it would overwhelm me, overtake me, and
swallow me whole. Yet running away from it was actually causing
my fears to come true.

It was time to take God's hand and knowing He was with me, stop running, turn, and face the pain. I surrendered myself to Him and asked Him for the courage I knew I would need. Everything in me wanted to run, yet I knew He wanted me to stand.

In facing the pain of what you've been through, the Lord will hold your hand, even carry you at times. When you face it instead of running, when you give release to the feelings and enter the process of forgiveness, you will not be alone. God will walk with you through it, caring for you, and helping you grow stronger. With His help, you will soar above the pain of the past, and He will do a beautiful work in you.

You don't have to face the pain alone. God is with you and will help you. Stay near to Him during this time and let Him bring you to a place of peace.

PRAYER

Father God, help me know I can trust you. I give you the broken pieces of my heart and ask that you would put them back together. Help me to face the pain, walking through it with you, knowing that at times I will need to let you carry me. I surrender the pain to you, and I release it into your hands. Give me the courage to feel, to stay in this process, and not turn and run. In Jesus' name, amen.

DAY 58

He Sees Your Tears

Put my tears into your bottle; are they not in your book?
—Psalm 56:8

I wondered why God would let this happen. I was going through hell on earth. Why didn't He stop it?

I would get away by myself and let the tears flow freely. And then, after I was done, I would put the mask back on that I wore for everyone else—the mask that said they had not broken me, they had not hurt me, and they hadn't brought me down. I hid my pain beneath a smile when I would have rather cried.

I knew God cared for He Himself ministered to me in my own prayer time and encouraged me not to give up. But the situation kept going on and on. When would it ever end?

These questions reeled through my mind, until one day I received prayer in a community of people who walked with God. The man who prayed for me placed his hand on my head and said, "Lord, you have seen her tears . . ."

That prayer confirmed to me, that God had seen my pain. He was listening to my prayers. He was walking through this terrible time with me, and I wasn't alone.

Have you cried out to God and wondered if He even heard you or if He even cares?

He has seen your tears, He has heard your cry, and He knows what you have been through because He's walked through it with you.

Do not give up hope! Giving up is exactly what the enemy of your soul wants you to do. He would like nothing better than for you to let yourself sink into despair.

Do not give him the satisfaction. Your answer is coming; it's on its way.

This pain will not last forever. Declare that you will not quit, that your hope is in the Lord of Lords and King of Kings who will never fail you (Zeph. 3:5).

Whenever you feel like giving up, cry out to God one more time. Spend time in worship and prayer. Open the book of Psalms and pray along with them. The Psalms are one of the greatest places to go when you are suffering and don't know how to pray.

Ask the Lord for encouragement not to give up hope and to keep moving forward. He will answer. He is faithful and will never abandon you.

PRAYER

Lord, help me not to give up. Encourage me by your spirit and help me live out each day, walking in the light of your promises. Strengthen me while I wait patiently for you. In Jesus' name, amen.

DAY 59

Your Father Loves You

The Lord has appeared of old to me, saying: "Yes, I have loved
you with an everlasting love; therefore with lovingkindness I
have drawn you."

—Jeremiah 31:3

I heard His voice clearly.

Most days in Bible college we started with chapel. That day,
a guest speaker spoke on how the Holy Spirit could work in our
lives. He described how he had entered into ministry and the ways
in which the Holy Spirit had shown up.

I could feel the excitement in the room. What more do Bible
college students want than to go into ministry and see signs and
wonders—tangible evidence of God's mercy and love?

I, however, sometimes wondered why I was even there. I'd come
to Bible college at God's leading, and He had confirmed that He
wanted me there several times. But it seemed everyone else was
there to learn how to minister to others, while I just wanted God's
healing for myself.

I knew my brokenness was evident to everyone around me,
and at times I felt as if I stuck out like a sore thumb—the one who
was not like the others.

So that day as I watched everyone else get excited about
ministering to others, I only wanted God to minister to me. The
man who spoke started praying for each of the students.

When he got to me, he laid his hand on my shoulder and prayed. I felt myself falling over, but I tried to stay standing. I had told God a long time before that I was not going to fall over just because. If He wanted to work that way in me, He would have to knock me off my feet.

And that is what He did.

I felt someone catch me from behind, and slowly I sank to the floor, overcome by the presence of the Lord. And that's when I heard Him speaking clearly to me.

"I love you. I love you. I love you. I love you."

I kept hearing those words over and over in my spirit. And as if God could not say it enough, the guest speaker knelt down next to my ear and said, "Your Father loves you! Do you hear your Father's voice?"

And that day, a day that I had started out feeling too broken to be of use to God, He knocked me off my feet and declared His love for me.

God doesn't look at you through the eyes of man. He sees what's inside of you. Man sees the outward manifestation of your brokenness, but God sees a heart that He can put back together. He sees the work He can do in you as if it's already done, since He sees the end from the beginning (Isa. 46:10). He has a plan to turn the ashes and broken pieces of your life into something beautiful.

There is no such thing as too broken for God. There is only Him, sweeping you off your feet and declaring His love for you.

PRAYER

Lord, I receive your love for me. I declare that I am your child. I am valuable and loved by my heavenly Father. Lord, I give you every broken piece of my life and trust you to make it into something beautiful. In Jesus' name, amen.

DAY 60

God Believes in You

For a great and effective door has opened to me, and there are
many adversaries.
—1 Corinthians 16:9

Paul spoke of an effective door opening for him with many adversaries. Wouldn't it be nice if God just opened doors, and you could easily step through them without any struggle?

Yet it seems that when the enemy sees a Christian moving forward with the Lord, he does whatever he can to put a stop to it. He will distract, discourage, and even influence people to do his work for him.

When I started getting serious about my walk with God and stepping out into the things He led me to do, the enemy used people around me to speak discouragement, to wound, and to bruise. They didn't see how God could possibly use me. It didn't fit their definition of me.

In the midst of all this painful discouragement, I sat in Bible class one day, and the teacher told the story of a time that someone in her life was coming against her. She said she finally had to stand up to this person and say directly to them, "You do not define me."

When you start taking your walk with God seriously, there are some who may be offended by it. It may not fit their definition of you, or it may make them uncomfortable with something in their own lives.

Whatever the reasons behind trying to dissuade and discourage, remember that it is not up to them to define you. It is up to God.

Don't let the enemy steal God's best by using people who don't believe in you. God believes in you. He knows you can do exactly what He has called you to do because He Himself will be doing it through you.

The Lord is not looking for a perfect vessel. He is looking for someone who is willing.

PRAYER

Lord, I forgive those who have defined me as someone who can't. I break the power of their definition of me, and I ask that you would help me to see myself as you see me. Help me to grow strong and mature in you. In Jesus' name, amen.

DAY 61

The Whole Table

You prepare a table before me in the presence of my enemies;
You anoint my head with oil; My cup runs over.
—Psalm 23:5

I sat quietly in the prayer room at church as worship music played softly in the background. Others prayed around me, and the presence of the Lord seemed tangible in that moment. My eyes were closed, and I focused on my Savior.

In the Spirit, I saw myself sitting at a table. I could only see in front of me, and I knew I was waiting for a plate. Then a light shone so I could see the rest of what was around me. The table I sat at was long; I couldn't see the end of it. And instead of the plate I had been waiting for, this table was filled with a feast.

I had only been waiting for a plate, but God had so much more for me.

When you have been hurt, wounded, and bruised on the inside, often you feel inferior. You can feel as if you don't want to get your hopes up too high or expect too much and more often than not, you are afraid to hope.

So much has been stolen from you already. Often your dignity, self-worth, and a feeling of physical safety has been threatened. So it is hard to hope for anything good.

God understands this. He knows what you've been through and sees the anguish in your soul (Ps. 31:7). But He wants to give you

121

so much more than just a plate. He's got a whole table for you. He wants to restore to you all the years the locusts have eaten (Joel 2:25). He wants to give you a double blessing for each of your troubles (Zech. 9:12).

You are not inferior, and you are not deserving of less than everyone else. You are valuable, loved, and adored by your heavenly Father. Look to Him and give Him your broken heart today. Ask Him to begin the process of healing in you.

It's time to hope again.

PRAYER

Jesus, I give you my heart, and I ask for your help in trusting you. Lead me and guide me in the way I should go and give me the courage to hope again. In Jesus' name, amen.

DAY 62

Wiping Ugly Words Away

For assuredly, I say to you, if you have faith as a mustard seed,
you will say to this mountain, "Move from here to there," and
it will move; and nothing will be impossible for you.

—Matthew 17:20

Someone had spoken words over me that hurt. They also made me angry, and I was having a hard time letting go. I spent my days offended, unable to stop thinking about these ugly words.

During this time, we visited a church where a family member was speaking. I went but with these words still hanging on me.

As the church entered into worship, I was whisked into the presence of God. After a few minutes, I had my eyes closed, singing to my heavenly Father, and it felt like it was just Him and me in that room.

That's when He showed me a picture of the words that were spoken, stuck to me, hanging off of my clothes as if someone had Velcroed them there. And He instructed me to wipe them away.

I tried to be inconspicuous and not draw too much attention to myself, while I brushed those words off of me with my hand like I was brushing something off of my clothes.

And I felt them go.

After suffering many days with these words hanging on me, I walked out of that church free of them. I had brushed them off and they weren't there anymore. I never struggled with those words again.

Are you struggling with words that have been spoken over you? Do you feel that they are just hanging on you, and you can't get rid of them?

I encourage you to get into the Lord's presence through worship, and while you worship, speak to those words. Tell them you don't receive them. Forgive the person who spoke them and then physically wipe them away.

Those ugly words do not need to torment you anymore.

PRAYER

In the name of Jesus, I forgive _____ for speaking hurtful words over me. I wipe those words away now in Jesus' name. You ugly words, I break your power over me now, and I no longer allow your hold on me. I tell you to go, in Jesus' name. Amen.

DAY 63

A Reminder of His Goodness

That they may set their hope in God, and not forget the works
of God, but keep his commandments;
—Psalm 78:7

Our family was in chaos.
Someone else's decisions were wreaking havoc on all of
us. Heartbroken, we could only watch from afar as this person
seemed intent on destroying themselves. We saw God give them
ways out, and we even tried to help them, only to have it thrown
back in our faces.

We all struggled through this time. We had to forgive, set
boundaries, and we had to let go of anger and fear, surrendering
this person to God. We felt as if our hearts were on the floor, broken
and shattered.

During this time, we attended a church retreat, and I asked for
prayer about this very situation. The woman I prayed with seemed
to listen to the Lord for a moment, then looked me straight in the
eye and said with such firmness and clarity, "He did it for you, and
He'll do it for them."

This woman had no idea what the Lord had brought me
through, no inkling of my story. I knew the Lord had spoken.

Hope rose within me. I started to think on what I had gone
through and how the Lord picked me up and put me back together

again. And I knew He could do that for this person too. I only needed to watch and pray and let Him fight the battle.

When you are going through trying times, remember on purpose what the Lord has already brought you through. He loves you so much, and He won't leave you here.

He'll bring you through this storm too. Lift your eyes to Jesus; He will not let you down. He is faithful.

PRAYER

Lord, I've been scared, lonely, and afraid. The storm has seemed so much bigger than me at times. Help me to remember that it is not bigger than you. Remind me of the good you've already done and give me an assurance that you won't leave me here. In Jesus' name, amen.

DAY 64

Keep Planting His Word

So shall My word be that goes forth from My mouth; It shall
not return to Me void, but it shall accomplish what I please,
and it shall prosper in the thing for which I sent it.
—Isaiah 55:11

It was the ugliest place to plant tulips, but I was tired of looking
at the never-ending weeds and gravel that lined our front fence.
Inside, our yard was beautiful, but we had never been able to get
past the rocky soil and clay in the front. It was an eyesore I didn't
know what to do with.

I had some extra bulbs that wouldn't fit in my garden. Instead
of putting them aside, I decided to plant them in the gravel against
the front fence. I imagined driving up to our house and instead of
seeing the weeds that were constantly poking through, I would be
looking at a touch of color and the beauty of those flowers instead.

I knew their chances of growing there were slim, but what else
was I going to do with them? I could always hope.

My husband walked by while I struggled in the rocky clay to
make holes big enough for the bulbs.

"That's not a good place to plant those." He said.

"I know." I kept digging.

Finally, the last tulip bulb was planted, and I picked up my
shovel and went into the house. Winter came, and I forgot about
those bulbs laying beneath the gravel.

Then, in early spring, I walked outside to see little tulip stems peeking out. Gravel, weeds, and dead leaves surrounded them, but there they stood in great splendor. Those tulips continued to bloom and when I drove up to my house that year, instead of the mess I had been so frustrated with, I enjoyed the beauty of those tulips.

They don't always come up every year anymore, but there is one that somehow made it to my husband's parking spot in the gravel, and every spring it pops its head up to stand in splendor, greeting us with its beauty in the midst of the mess and reminding me that even out of the worst mess, God can make something beautiful.

When things in our lives seem hopeless, lift them up to God. Give them over to Him in prayer every time the thought of it comes to mind. Plant the seed of God's Word deep within your heart, keeping it in your eyes and in your ears, speaking it aloud on a regular basis. Do not let go of the hope that God will work in your situation even when you don't see anything yet.

One day, when you least expect it, you will realize God has taken that mess you gave to Him and turned it into something beautiful.

PRAYER

Lord, I give you my mess. I hold it up to you now and declare that you are bigger than this mess, bigger than all my heartache and pain. Give me the strength and encouragement to hope in you, to keep planting your Word in my heart. Help me to remember that your Word will not return to you void but will do what you've called it to do. Lord, take this mess and make it something beautiful. In Jesus' name, amen.

DAY 65

Jesus Is Greater

You are of God, little children, and have overcome them,
because He who is in you is greater than he who is in the world.
—1 John 4:4

I could feel it coming down the stairs.

My husband had left for his graveyard shift an hour before, and my children slept upstairs. I sat alone in the living room, enjoying some time to myself.

The enjoyment quickly turned to fear when I felt a big ball of ugliness creeping toward me. I cannot explain exactly what it was, except to say that it was a big blob of everything bad: fear, anger, darkness, despair, and torment all wrapped up together into one ugly thing that I could not see with my eyes but sensed distinctly.

It came closer.

Moving slowly, it closed the space between us until I feared it would overtake me. Fear had left me frozen, unable to speak or move, but in my mind I cried out, "Help me Jesus!"

Immediately a Scripture I recently memorized came pouring out of my mouth without me even thinking about it.

In that instant, that big blob of darkness turned around and left. God's Word had repelled it from me.

Even when you are so afraid that you've lost your ability to react physically, you can still cry out to Jesus in your mind. You have the greater one living on the inside of you, and at your cry, He answers.

Keep your eyes and your ears attuned to God's Word. Stay close to Him in worship and prayer. Spend time with Him daily.

At just the right time, that Word you have been putting in your heart will come to mind or pouring out of your mouth without you even thinking about it. It will repel the enemy out of your life and help you walk in the peace of God.

PRAYER

Jesus, help me to grasp the greatness of your presence in my life—that you abide within me. Protect me, Lord, from the attacks of the enemy. Where darkness would try to make its way into my life and steal my peace, fill my mouth with your Word, repelling the darkness from me. Deliver me from every fear that tries to hold me captive. Help me to know who I am in you and the authority I have through your name. In Jesus' name, amen.

DAY 66

You Matter

You are the light of the world.
—Matthew 5:14

A box of donated books sat on the counter.
All the kids gathered around and grabbed one. I was the last one to get my book, and there was only one left.

The Bible.

I reached in, took it, and started toward my room.

An older boy who looked on with the others said, "Don't you know that's the Bible?"

"I know." I made a point not to look at him as I walked by.

That night, in a dimly lit, sparse room, I opened that Bible and read. Words of life, hope, and comfort came off those pages and jumped into my heart. After much trauma and away from my family, I held in my hands a Bible that someone had lovingly donated to a traumatized teenager who felt very alone.

You may not know what God does with your prayers or even with a small act of kindness. But every time you pray and every time you follow the leading of the Lord, you are making a difference in this dark world, shining the light of Jesus like a candle showing the way home.

Through your prayers and your kindness, Jesus is giving someone hope today. You matter; you are very significant. You are a light shining brightly for the kingdom of God.

PRAYER

In the name of Jesus, I break the power of the lie that has told me I was insignificant and that my prayers did not matter. I break that lie off of my mind now, and I declare that every one of my prayers matters, making a difference in someone's life. Father, encourage me in my prayers and small acts of kindness and show me how significant they are to you, to others, and to your kingdom. In Jesus' name, amen.

DAY 67

Hang On and Trust God

Be still, and know that I am God; I will be exalted among the
nations, I will be exalted in the earth!

—Psalm 46:10

I have always hated roller coasters.

People tried to convince me that the ride would be fun, but
I knew what it really was: several minutes of pure terror. I have
happily sat on the sidelines while other people enjoyed a roller
coaster ride. They can have all the fun they want, but I will not
get on one.

Yet what about when life seems like a roller coaster, and you
can't decide if you want to get on or not because you're already
spiraling down a rough curve, holding on for dear life? You go down
fast, thinking everything is going to crash only to turn upwards
at the last minute, crawling so slowly toward the top you fear you
will never get there.

In these times, the Lord has always said, "Trust me."

Once I asked Him, "Lord, how do I trust you? I don't even
know how to trust anymore."

And the answer was to go spend time with Jesus in the Word,
worship, and prayer, getting to know Him better. I found myself
taking time to be quiet and still before Him, listening for what He
would speak to my heart.

Do not let go of what God has promised you. It may take some time to come to pass, and you may stay on the roller coaster ride longer than you want, but if you do not give up on what God has promised, you will see it come to pass.

Hang on and trust God.

PRAYER

Lord, teach me to trust you. I ask that you would heal the wounds in my heart that have caused me to not trust anymore. Show me how to trust again; help me to know in my heart that you are faithful, that you will never forsake me and never let me down. In Jesus' name, amen.

DAY 68

Planting Words

Pleasant words are like a honeycomb, sweetness to the soul
and health to the bones.

—Proverbs 16:24

Ever since we were children, we've had words spoken over us.
Some were words of encouragement to build up and empower.
Other words were not so nice: words of accusation, rejection, and
hatred.

And as each word was spoken, a seed was planted in our hearts.
If someone said we could do anything we put our mind to, we
believed we could. And if someone said we would never amount
to anything or called us names, sadly, those words were planted
in our hearts too.

I have had to do a lot of digging up and replanting in my life.
Weeds of words spoken over me years ago had almost taken over
the garden of my heart. But the Lord is a master gardener. He knows
how to take those ugly words out, and He has given us just the
seed to do it with.

When you plant what your heavenly Father says about you
in your heart, the seed of that Word immediately goes to work.
And if you keep planting it and watering that seed by reviewing
it regularly, you will eventually see truth begin to grow and bear
fruit in your life. For what you believe about yourself, affects the

way you view the world around you, how you react, and how you go about your daily life.

Plant the seed of God's Word in your heart today.

PRAYER

Lord, I ask your forgiveness for every negative word I have spoken about myself. And I forgive those who have spoken ungodly words over me, words that did not agree with what you have said. Show me who I am in you, Lord, and help me to receive your words for myself. I give you permission to begin weeding the garden of my heart. In Jesus' name, amen.

DAY 69

Freedom from Torment

And whenever you stand praying, if you have anything against
anyone, forgive him, that your Father in heaven may also
forgive you your trespasses.

—Mark 11:25

Our church had a pastor who told us that offenses could stick
to us like glue, or they could slide off of us like we were
nonstick pans.

I liked to think of myself more as a flower than a pan, though.

His point was that we choose whether to forgive or not.

Refusing to forgive lets the offense stick to you, keeping you
from growing, and it leaves you stuck in the quicksand of offense.

After a while, if you let it, that offense begins to fester. By
dwelling on it, it becomes bigger and bigger, wrapping itself around
you until all you are and all you were meant to be is covered by
that offense.

What a trap offense can be!

But when you choose to forgive, offense cannot do the damage it
could have otherwise done. By forgiving, you can move on, trusting
God to deal with the one who hurt you.

Forgiving is not always easy. If it were, everyone would do it.

It is a continual letting go of the hurt and pain by choice.

Every time the anger or the memory of what was done comes
to mind, lift your hands up to God is if you are handing it to Him.

Give Him that memory and all the emotions attached to it and declare you forgive the one who hurt you.

You may have to do this a lot at first, especially if you have been dwelling on the offense for a long time. But the more you do it and the longer you keep choosing to forgive, giving the memories and emotions over, you'll realize that you're thinking of the offense less and less. And one day, you will be completely free. You have forgiven.

You left the offense in God's hands, and you are free of the torment. The memory of what happened might still be there, but the emotions and hurt do not come with it anymore. No longer are you reliving the past pain every day of your life.

Forgiveness is not easy. It is a choice, and it *is* possible.

You can be tormented by the offense, letting it consume you, or you can continually offer it up to God, choosing to forgive until you are free.

PRAYER

Lord, I choose to forgive_____ for_____.
I release _____ into your hands, she/he is your burden now and not mine. Heal my heart, Lord, from all the hurt, pain, and torment. In Jesus' name, amen.

DAY 70

Sleep on It

When I remember You on my bed, I meditate on You in the
night watches.

—Psalm 63:6

I had the hardest time sleeping. It was torment, really, with things weighing so heavy on my heart and mind that I couldn't rest.

This went on for years.

Then during Bible college, our assignments often included reading large portions of Scripture at a time. I took my Bible to bed with me and read into the night, trying to get my reading assignments done.

And I noticed something.

When I read my Bible at night, I slept better. I went to sleep with God's promises on my heart and mind instead of all that was going on around and within me. Focusing on God gave me peace, and I was able to rest.

When you make it a habit to be in the Word, no matter what time of day, you will find comfort and strength. With God's Word on your mind and heart, you will be able to rest in Him.

Open up the Word of God before you go to bed tonight. Highlight key verses that speak to your heart. Read for as little or as long as you like. Then fall asleep with God's promises on your mind.

PRAYER

Lord, speak to me through your Word, keep me in perfect peace as I meditate on your Word. May your truth break through every lie, every fear and permeate my mind until it is overflowing with your truth. In Jesus' name, amen.

DAY 71

Why?

The thief does not come except to steal, and to kill, and to
destroy. I have come that they may have life, and that they may
have it more abundantly.

—John 10:10

The battle was long and hard. I was weary, questioning God's
love and why He would let this awful thing happen to me.

"Why?" was a question I asked a lot.

I felt an answer came when I asked a woman to pray for me. I
told her I didn't want to share the whole situation but asked if she
would just pray what God put on her heart.

She prayed and then paused, saying, "Lord, I pray that this,
whatever this is, would never happen to her again. Don't let it *ever*
happen again, Lord."

I do not remember the rest of what she prayed, but those words
were burned into my mind forever.

Another lady who prayed for me about the same situation said,
"The enemy is using their weaknesses to get to you . . ."

I felt the Lord was showing me that this wasn't what His will was for
me, this situation wasn't His plan, and He didn't do it. He was showing
me that He would take me through this pain and heartache, and He
wanted to heal me of the damage done to me through what happened.

The Lord has good plans for you. He came to give you abundant
life.

When you and I have suffered at the hands of someone else, sometimes it is hard to see the light at the end of the tunnel. We ask questions of God. We question His love for us.

This is exactly what the enemy would have you do. He wants you to question God's love, question the integrity of God's Word, and if he can, get you to quit, to walk away from God altogether.

The enemy wants to leave you wounded, bruised, broken, offended, and bitter. He wants to torment you for the rest of your life.

But this is not what God wants for you.

God understands what you have gone through. He understands perfectly suffering at the hands of others. He understands your broken heart, your anger, and your pain.

And He wants to help you heal. He wants to help you forgive, to let go of the anguish, and trust Him to deal with what happened to you.

He wants to unburden you, so you can walk upright again, free of all that the enemy has tried to burden you with.

Your heavenly Father wants to take you out of the ashes of abuse, hurt, anger, shame, and trauma. He wants to heal you, heal your heart, and give you a life free from torment and emotional pain.

He has seen everything you've gone through. He has seen every tear you have ever cried. And He has been with you through all of it.

Your heavenly Father wants to deliver you from the pain and suffering, and He wants to give you life.

PRAYER

Lord, this hurt and pain is so heavy at times. Sometimes I feel I can hardly go on. I give you permission to come into my heart and start unburdening me. I give you the shame, anger, and rejection. I give you the unforgiveness and offense. I ask you, Father, to come and heal my heart. You know exactly what I need. Unwrap every offense, every darkness, every anger, every pain, and free me from the trap of the enemy. In Jesus' name, amen.

DAY 72

Fill Your Cup

And when He had sent the multitudes away, He went up on
the mountain by Himself to pray. Now when evening came, He
was alone there.

—Matthew 14:23

Several family crises had come up in a very short time. Family
members were in the hospital, and I was asked to take care of
things while also trying to care for my own household.

The stress of it all weighed heavy on me as time went on, until
one day I took to my bed and pulled the covers up over my head.
Besides the things I was already giving, I had others who were also
asking for help. I kept hearing the message, "We need you. We need
your time, your talents, your money."

It got to the point that when I knew the can-you-help question
was coming, my stomach clenched.

And that day, in bed, I just cried. I couldn't give any more.

I talked with a counselor, who said, "Do you do anything for
you?"

The truth was, I hadn't in a long time. I'd wanted to, even
planned to, and then something else would come up.

I knew I couldn't keep this up anymore. I had to let some things
go and take time for myself. I needed to fill my own cup before
I poured out to anyone else. I was empty, feeling resentful, and
needed time for me.

143

As women, we can so easily let ourselves be taxed on every side until we take to our beds with nothing left to give.

Make sure you take time to fill your own cup. Schedule that time and don't let anyone make you feel guilty about it. It is not selfish; it is needed. You cannot give to someone else what you don't have yourself.

Love yourself today.

Do something nice for you.

PRAYER

Lord, I ask that you would help me take time for myself, to realize that loving myself is crucial and needed before I can love someone else. Help me to take care of myself and not feel guilty about it. In Jesus' name, amen.

DAY 73

Cling to Jesus

That he might sanctify and cleanse it with the washing of the
water by the word.
—Ephesians 5:26 KJV

As a young lady freshly out on my own without God, I began
running to people, thinking they would fill me. Relationships
became strained, and I enabled people because I was afraid they
wouldn't love me otherwise. I gave myself away, wanting to
somehow get the love I was starving for.

I ended up hurt, even more broken, and very disappointed.

God, in His love, drew me to Himself, and I started to lean on
Him instead of people. I was not automatically fixed by any means;
I had to go through a process of healing.

When you have been in unhealthy habits for a long time, it may
take some time to grow out of them. But with the Lord's help, you
can walk free of them.

Be patient with yourself. You haven't learned these things
overnight, and it will be a process to grow out of them.

Choose to love yourself right where you are, the way you are,
unhealthy habits and all. Memorize Scriptures on God's love for
you and repeat them to yourself daily. God's Word will go to work
in you, for it is living and active (Heb. 4:12).

When you are made aware that you are walking in an unhealthy way, take it to Jesus and give it to Him in prayer. Ask Him to help you become healthy.

It took years for God to work in me. It did not happen overnight, and He is still at work in me. But God is faithful. Continue in His Word. Continue in prayer, worship, and fellowshipping with other believers. God is working in you, and He will be faithful to complete the work He started (Phil. 1:6).

You are God's child, precious to Him (Deut. 7:6), the apple of His eye (Zech. 2:8). He will not leave you here. Take steps toward Him by being patient, giving Him your unhealthy habits, and asking Him to work in you.

He will not let you down.

PRAYER

Lord Jesus, I give you my unhealthy habits: the ones I know about and the ones I'm not aware of. I invite you to go to work in me. As I read your Word and pray, heal my heart and my life and show me the way that you would have me walk. Thank you Jesus, that you love me right where I am, the way I am, today, and that you, in your love and mercy, will set me free from unhealthy habits. In Jesus' name, amen.

# DAY 74

Freedom from Manipulating Powers

"For I know the plans I have for you," declares the LORD,
"plans to prosper you and not to harm you, plans to give you
hope and a future."
—Jeremiah 29:11 NIV

I had believed the lie for so long it had almost become a part of me. Someone in my life had me under their thumb; they cried and I responded. They called me with false expectations thinking I should meet their needs—needs I couldn't possibly be responsible for—yet I tried. I was destined to fail this person over and over, for they were putting all of their hopes in me, a very broken person who needed God myself.

Whenever I was around them, I felt drained and guilty for failing them once again. Their words hurt and sometimes pierced my very soul. I had little energy and was not taking care of myself. When I did try to take care of me, a phone call would come and even if this person didn't outright say it, their tone said it all. They were not pleased with me.

My life was like a yo-yo, going up and down with this person's emotions. I became angry, bitter, and tried not talking to them. It made them unhappier still, and they showed up at my front door with their demands.

Years went by.

I entered into the process of God's healing, and He had me limit my time with this person. And slowly, He helped me allow them back into my life. He led me to pray for this person and, at times, confront their behavior.

The more healing I received, the more I was able to love this person in healthy ways.

And one day, I was visiting with them, and we were playing a board game. I looked up at them, and this thought hit me with such clarity: *I am not responsible for your happiness.*

It was not a hateful thought but a freeing one. This person had tried to get from me what was missing in their life for so long, and the realization that I was not responsible for them freed me.

They were responsible for their own happiness, and nothing I could say or do was ever going to fill them. I could love them, keep healthy boundaries, and pray for them, but I could never fill them.

People may try and make you responsible for their happiness. They may frequently call you, make unhealthy demands, and try to manipulate you into doing what they want.

When this happens, you have a choice. You can either succumb to their demands and open it up to happen again, or you can take it to the Lord and ask Him to help you set healthy boundaries.

Seek His will for you in prayer. Ask for wisdom and maybe even seek out a trusted pastor or counselor to help you walk through this relationship.

What you are responsible for is your own relationship with God. He has created you with purposes and plans to fulfill. You were not created to make someone else happy but to walk in the purposes you were especially fashioned for.

PRAYER

Lord Jesus, I bring before you every unhealthy relationship in my life. Show me, Lord, that I am not responsible for other people's happiness. Help me to know what I am responsible for and what I am not responsible for. Show me how to have healthy, loving boundaries. Lord, I choose you. I choose not to be manipulated and controlled any longer, and I break the power of manipulation and control off my life right now, in Jesus' name. Lord, where I have opened doors to being manipulated, I pray that you would close those doors and bring healing to my life. I choose your plans and purposes for my life, and I will not be robbed of them anymore. In Jesus' name, amen.

DAY 75

Daily Encouragement

All Scripture is given by inspiration of God, and is profit-
able for doctrine, for reproof, for correction, for instruction
in righteousness,
—2 Timothy 3:16

I knew I should read my Bible. I'd been told that many times.
I held the book in my hands and had no idea where to start.
Someone had told me once to start in Matthew and work my
through from there, so I tried.

Distractions came. Confusion played with my mind, telling
me I didn't understand it or hadn't read the right part. I would
end up closing my Bible, discouraged. I felt alone and even a little
ashamed when I heard people talk about the Bible like they knew
it inside and out.

I wanted to know it like they did; I just didn't know how.

After much prayer, I made a decision to be in the Word of God
every day no matter if I understood it or not. I ordered a book on
how to study the Bible and started putting what I learned into
practice.

After only a few months of making that quality decision to be
in the Word, I realized I understood it better, and it was speaking
to my heart.

Today I read the Bible on a daily basis and even if I don't get
something out of it every day, that's OK. Most days I do. I made

that quality decision a long time ago, and reading the Word of God every day has affected every area of my life.

When you pick up a Bible for the first time and don't know where to start, it can be overwhelming. But there are some things you can do to make the habit of reading your Bible less of a challenge.

Make a quality decision that you will do it every day and be consistent. Choose beforehand what you will read. There are several Bible reading plans available online that you can choose from. Pick a time that works for you and mark that time on your calendar. As you read, journal what you feel the Lord is speaking to your heart.

Invite the Holy Spirit to minister to your heart as you read. The Word of God will encourage you, guide you, and correct you. After a while, reading it daily will affect every area of your life. It will feed your spirit and uplift your soul.

Before I made daily Bible reading a habit, I let my emotions rule me. I believed in Jesus as my Savior, but there was no lasting growth in my life. As I grew more in the knowledge of God's Word, I started to mature, and my emotions ruled less and less.

Daily Bible reading can become a part of your life. I encourage you to make that decision to be in the Word daily; it will change your life for the better.

PRAYER

Lord, I ask that you would minister to my heart as I read your Word. Give me an understanding and a love for your Word. Let it speak to my heart, my mind, and to the wounds within my soul. Let me find daily encouragement in you. In Jesus' name, amen.

DAY 76

Healing from Depression

I will be glad and rejoice in your love, for you saw my afflic-
tion and knew the anguish of my soul.
—Psalm 31:7 NIV

The conversation I overheard reminded me of my own struggle
with depression.

I was in the grocery store, looking toward the meat counter. A
woman stood near me, talking to the clerk who seemed to know
her.

"How are you today?" the clerk asked.

"I am so depressed; I don't even know why I'm here anymore."
She answered.

The conversation continued, and as I moved away, I said a
prayer that the Lord would give her joy and a purpose.

I left the store thinking of my own struggle with depression.
At one time I had wondered the same thing. What was the point
of everything I had gone through? Why was I even here?

Why did I hurt so bad inside? Would I ever get through it? I
didn't see an end to the pain. Waves of emotion swept over me,
and sometimes I wondered if they would engulf me altogether.

When you are hurting, you may not be able to see a way out of
the hurt. It may feel like it will go on forever. You may be plagued
with questions about your purpose: why you are here, why you

have suffered so, and why do you hurt so badly? But there is a way out of the pain; there is a way out of depression.

I have been so depressed I could not get out of bed and was even hospitalized for it at one point. I didn't want to live anymore. I thought the pain was all there was.

I know that the depression and the pain seem so big right now. But there is someone bigger than all of that pain. He is bigger than that depression, and He will help you overcome. He will lift you out of the hurt and brokenness. He will give you strength to get through the next minute, the next hour, the next day. He will help you find joy.

Depression does not need to rule your life anymore.

By an act of your will, get up and get dressed. Put on some lipstick.

Get yourself a cup of coffee or tea and sit down with the Lord. Put on some worship music if you have it or find a good Christian radio station.

You may not feel like singing at all but by an act of your will, decide to sing. Decide to worship the Lord for a while. You may be tired; it may take a lot of energy. Don't let that stop you.

After you have sung a few songs, go outside and sit for a while if the weather permits. If it's sunny, let yourself bask in its warmth.

Thank the Lord for the sunshine.

Thank Him that you are alive today and that you have hope.

Thank Him for the cup of tea or coffee you are holding.

Just sit with Him a while, thinking of things you can be thankful for. Your mind might not want to go there. Go to that place of thankfulness anyway. Anything you can find, thank Him for it. Thank Him for the air, the grass, the bed you sleep in. Thank Him for hot water. Whatever you can think of, thank Him for it.

Now go get your Bible. Open it and read for just a little while. You don't have to read for a long time.

Is there a promise the Lord is speaking to you?

Close your eyes and think on that promise. Talk to God about it.

If you need to cry, allow yourself to do so. Jesus is with you, and you are not alone.

God has a purpose for you. He wants to heal the pain in your heart. He wants to lift you from that emotional pain and depression and restore you to a place of joy.

It may look like a long way off but know that it's not too far.

You will get there.

You will smile again.

You will feel happiness again.

God will not leave you here. You are not alone.

He is not mad at you for being depressed. He loves you dearly, knows your name, hears your heart's cry, and wants to set you free.

PRAYER

Lord, I thank you that you know the pain in my heart; you know my struggles Lord, and you do not condemn me for them, but you are full of compassion for me. You love me, and you want to set me free. I lay myself before you, Father God, and I invite you in to heal my life. Help me to live again. Help me, Lord, to take the next breath, and know that you are with me. Give me the strength to face the next minute, Lord. I cry out to you and ask for your healing. In Jesus' name, amen.

DAY 77

Do You Love Me?

To know the love of Christ which passes knowledge; that you
may be filled with all the fullness of God.

—Ephesians 3:19

That niggling wonder.

"God loves you Carolyn," someone would say.

I nodded as if I already knew but really, I wondered. There was
a part of me that *wanted* to believe God loved me, but another,
bigger part wondered if He really did at all.

If He loves me so much, why did these things happen to me?

Every time someone spoke of God's love for me, I agreed with
my mind but deep down in my heart, I didn't believe I was worthy
of God's love. I didn't think about or compare His love for other
people, I just knew *I* didn't feel worthy.

I have found that people who have been through much trauma,
who've suffered at the hands of others or experienced great loss,
often question God's love and feel unworthy or inferior to others. I
just happened to be one of those who felt unworthy, and the enemy
was having a heyday!

I was angry, hurt, wounded, and struggled with rejection and
my own self-worth. To top it all off, I wondered if anyone in this
world really loved me at all, let alone God. I felt empty and alone.

I felt I had to somehow earn the love I wanted from others. I let
people walk all over me because maybe they would love me then,
when the truth was, God already loved me.

The problem wasn't Gods love for me: He declared His love from the foundation of the world (Eph. 1:4) and sent Jesus to die on the cross for me. The problem was that I felt so unworthy of God's love, I couldn't receive it, and it was affecting every area of my life.

Receiving God's love for you can be a major part of your healing and restoration. When you believe that God loves you, you will feel more secure, be more sure of yourself, and walk in more freedom.

For me, this has been a lifetime assignment. Receiving God's love for me has been a process: I grow a little more in knowing His love and then realize I need to know more of it. Little by little, step by step, I keep growing in God's love.

You can overcome that feeling of unworthiness and receive God's love for you. Be mindful of little things He does for you throughout the day and thank Him for those things.

Memorize and think on Scriptures regarding God's love for you. There are a whole lot in the Bible to choose from. When I keep my eyes on Scriptures about God's love for me, I am noticeably more secure and sure of myself.

Soon, the truth of God's love for you will break through all the pain you've carried for so long. You'll start walking a little taller and when someone says God loves you, it won't be hard to believe anymore.

Keep your mind on God's love for you and continue to receive His love. You will begin the process of growing in His love, be more sure of yourself, and better able to love others with the love the Holy Spirit has shed abroad in your heart (Rom. 5:5).

PRAYER

Lord, as an act of my will, I choose to receive your love for me. I invite you into every place in my heart where I have questioned whether you love me or not. Clean out the rejection, the hurt, and the pain. Help me to be mindful of your love and continue to grow in the knowledge of your love for me. Help me, Lord, to see myself as you see me and to know that I am precious, loved, and valued in your sight. In Jesus' name, amen.

DAY 78

The Way Out Is Through

I called on the Lord in distress; the Lord answered me and set
me in a broad place.
—Psalm 118:5

I spent many days broken and hurting, crying out for the hurt to
go away. So many days I suffered pain and anguish. I couldn't get
away from it but carried it everywhere I went. Nothing I could buy,
no where I could go made it any better. No relationship filled me.

The hurt and pain sat in my heart, and I needed to face it, but
I didn't want to. Though I was tormented by it, I didn't actually
want to take it out and look at it.

What if I wasn't fixable? What if the pain was so great I couldn't
stop feeling it? What if I let it out, and it overtook me? I thought it
was better bottled up, hidden. That way I could control it.

What I didn't realize is what I had bottled up seeped out in
different ways. I got sick easier, and it took me longer to get better.
I was stressed, unable to sleep, easily offended, and was quick to
cry or get angry about little things.

Slowly, gently, the Lord led me to face the pain.

Tears came that had been bottled up for years. When I had
held them back as a child, they only built up within me and still
needed to be let out. I grieved the things that happened to me and
wrote pages and pages in my journals. I talked with trusted people,
received prayer for healing, and became brutally honest with God.

157

I didn't hold back when I shared my feelings with Him. Nor did I hold back the questions I had for Him.

How I wished I could have felt that pain and had it be over in a day!

But no, first I opened my heart to the Lord, and He started with one thing. I cried, I grieved, I forgave. I let myself feel the feelings. I wrote about what happened to me in a private journal.

Then He started with the next thing.

I needed to process the pain in my heart, and it took time. And I will tell you, it took courage and guts. It was not easy.

I let myself feel the anger and pain, I cried, I screamed into pillows. I wept till no more tears would come. And then I looked to God.

I received His comfort and love and with His help, I forgave. It was a process, and my heavenly Father walked with me through all of it. He never left me.

I could not walk through the pain quickly. But with each day that I let myself cry, let myself feel, I was one day closer to freedom.

Don't believe the lie that you will never be free, that you will never be able to stop crying, or that you will always have to live with the pain.

You can walk into freedom.

But first you must walk through the pain. Stop avoiding it and let yourself feel. Give yourself permission to cry. Let it out. Tell God how you feel. Pray. Journal. Seek out a counselor, trusted friend, or pastor.

You will be able to stop crying. You will be able to walk through this. It won't be easy. It will take courage and a dependence on God. Each day you will be one step closer to freedom and one day, the memories will be there, but the pain and anguish will not. You will be free.

PRAYER

Lord, give me the courage to face this pain. Help me to face it and deal with it in the time that it takes for me. I pray that you would walk through it with me, guide me, comfort me, and show me how to forgive and how to grieve and not keep holding it in. Help me to heal. Put trustworthy people around me to help me walk through this. In Jesus' name, amen.

DAY 79

The Broken Pieces

For I am persuaded that neither death nor life, nor angels nor
principalities nor powers, nor things present nor things to
come, nor height nor depth, nor any other created thing, shall
be able to separate us from the love of God which is in Christ
Jesus our Lord.

—Romans 8:38–39

The pain in my heart overwhelmed me. How come I had to go
through all of this? Why did these things happen to me? Hadn't
God promised me *good* things?

Where were they?

I wanted to give up, to sit down and not go on one more
moment. Yet I knew, somehow, that would not be a good decision.

God's promises seemed so far off, unreachable. Yet through the
comfort of His love, He encouraged me to go on just one more day
and then another.

You can question God and be sorrowing deeper than you ever
have before. You can be in the worst emotional pain you could
imagine, and yet it cannot separate you from God's love.

He cries with you and wants to put every broken piece back
together again. He sees the things you've been through, what you're
going through right this moment, and He wants to heal your heart.

Openly cry your tears out to Him. Tell Him how you feel and
ask for His comfort. He is listening, and He is there with you right

now. God is not an absentee father but an ever-present one who cares so deeply for you.

Picture yourself in your heavenly Father's hands. Let yourself rest there a while. Know that He loves you like no one else ever could. And though others have failed you, He will never fail you (Deut. 31:6). You are safe in His hands and nothing can snatch you out of them (John 10:29).

Sit with Him and give Him each tear, every wound, bruise, and callous, every situation that has broken your heart. Ask Him to bring you to a place of healing.

When you are in the midst of suffering, it's hard to see how God could make anything beautiful out of what you've been through. It's OK. Give it to Him anyway. He will show you how as He does it, and one day you will look back with great joy in your heart and tell about the wonderful work He has done in you.

PRAYER

Lord, I pray that you would take every broken piece of my heart and knit it back together. I can't hold it together anymore; I am broken and unable to do this on my own. I put these pieces into your hands and release them to you now. Help me to rest in your love. Help me to know it's OK not to be OK. I can come to you and give you my tears, my anger, and my pain. Help me to know you are an ever-present, loving Father and that you will walk with me through this pain into the good things you have for me. In Jesus' name, amen.

DAY 80

No More Torment

Finally, brothers and sisters, whatever is true, whatever is
noble, whatever is right, whatever is pure, whatever is lovely,
whatever is admirable—if anything is excellent or praisewor-
thy—think about such things.
—Philippians 4:8 NIV

As an adult, I wish I had told someone. But as a child, I didn't
question her cruel words. Instead, I believed them.

I stepped onto the school bus with everyone else after school
that day. Slowly, I made my way up the big stairs until I came face
to face with the driver.

She looked down at me from her big chair and instead of a
kind face, her lips curled down. She looked like a dog that was
about to snarl.

As I passed by her, she whispered, "You're the ugliest."

I said nothing and found my window seat. Holding back tears,
I stared out at the world going by around me. Then I went home
where the world didn't seem any better.

As children we believe what we are told about ourselves, good
or bad. We don't know how to filter out the bad from the good. If
someone says it, it must be true. What we hear as children shapes
our world and how we see ourselves.

161

Words written on our hearts can play over and over again in our minds long into adulthood. Words spoken years before still have the power to pierce our souls as if they were spoken yesterday.

What is written on your heart?

You don't have to let ugly words someone spoke to you as a child run rampant through your mind anymore. You can stop them from hurting you ever again. The sting of those words can be replaced with the truth of God's Word about you.

What is the lie you were told?

Is the lie that you were ugly? The Lord says you are beautiful (Song 4:7).

Is the lie that you are not worth much? The Lord says you are His treasure (Deut. 7:6).

Is the lie that you are not lovable? The Lord says He died for you because He loves you so much (John 3:16).

For every lie, there is a truth in God's Word that will overpower it. Whenever the lie comes to mind, start speaking the truth of God's Word. Look at that truth in the morning and at night before you go to bed. Keep speaking the truth until the lie doesn't come around anymore.

What you believe about yourself affects the way you act, the way you respond, and even how you hold and carry yourself. Knowing and believing the truth about yourself will set you free, allowing you to walk in peace.

The lies will not be able to torment you anymore.

PRAYER

In the name of Jesus, I break the power of the lies that have been spoken over me. I bind that lying spirit in Jesus' name and tell it to flee far from me. You will no longer have reign over my mind. I declare that I have the mind of Christ. I am free from torment now in Jesus' name. Amen.

DAY 81

Overcoming Doubt

For our struggle is not against flesh and blood, but against
the rulers, against the authorities, against the powers of
this dark world and against the spiritual forces of evil in the
heavenly realms.

—Ephesians 6:12 NIV

"And we come against the spirit of doubt right now," the woman
prayed.

I hadn't told her I'd been struggling with that. But the Lord
knew. I'd come so far. So much healing had already been done. I
had seen God's power in my life; I had experienced His deliverance
in myself and others.

And yet, I doubted He would work in *this* situation.

The mountain was bigger than me, and the situation had been
going on for a long time. I spent many days crying out to God,
asking Him, "When? When are you going to deliver me? When
are you going to come? When, Lord, when?"

A year went by, two, then three.

Discouragement came, and tied to it was doubt—doubt that
God was ever going to move and a fear that I would always be
waiting.

When the woman prayed, I felt something stir inside of me.
Doubt was leaving. It had covered my hope and closed the curtains
on believing God's Word but no more. After that prayer, I was

able to go to God's Word and plant it in my heart once again. And instead of doubt, faith grew.

When things get tough and go on for a long time, discouragement can set in and along with it, doubt, fear, depression, anger, and anxiety. It doesn't show itself for what it is until it's nice and settled in, and one day you wake up and wonder where all your trust in the Lord went.

You realize it's gone.

Though discouragement and doubt may come, you don't have to stay there. There is a way out, and you can hope again. You can get up and open the curtains to faith, belief, and trust again.

Start speaking to the doubt. Speak directly to it and tell it to get out of your life in Jesus' name. Fill your mind with God's promise about your situation. Speak that promise out loud and hang on to it with all your might.

You might fall into the trap of letting your emotions take over once in a while. Don't let that stop you. Tell God you're sorry and move on. Don't beat yourself up; God will help you overcome this if you ask Him.

Grab onto that promise again. Keep it in front of you, putting it into your eyes, your ears, and your mouth.

Hope will rise. Faith will rise.

And even though you may wait longer than you want to, the mountain that was in front of you will fall, and you will walk over it like it was only a pebble.

PRAYER

Lord, I ask your forgiveness for every time I have let my emotions rule. I ask for your help, Lord, to overcome doubt and fear and to not let them stop me anymore. I choose you, Lord. I choose your Word, and I choose to believe your promise to me. Encourage and comfort me; give me strength while I wait upon you. In Jesus' name, amen.

DAY 82

You Are Valuable

But you are a chosen generation, a royal priesthood, a holy
nation, His own special people, that you may proclaim the
praises of Him who called you out of darkness into His
marvelous light.

—1 Peter 2:9

I sat in a chair with my Bible and a journal, while my son watched
cartoons. Quietly I read and came upon a verse that spoke to my
heart. As I stopped and meditated on it for a few moments, I started
to pour out my heart to the Lord in my mind and on the page.

I felt inferior. I felt that something must be wrong with me for
people to treat me as they had. I believed this so strongly that I
started apologizing to God for being inferior.

The response that came to my heart and spirit was strong,
commanding. "You were never inferior! Don't ever believe that! I
created you, and I do not create inferior things!"

I sat for a moment.

I was just a little bit stunned. For most of my life I believed I
was less than in some way, that it must be the reason people treated
me so. And God said I wasn't.

That belief system did not go away overnight. But the Lord took
it away as I grew in Him, and He worked healing in me. I learned
to accept that what happened to me was not my fault. The way

people treated me was because of them not because I had done something wrong.

I was not inferior in any way.

It is so easy to fall into the enemy's trap when you have suffered at the hands of others. He leads you to believe that you have done something wrong, that you deserved it in some way. He wants you to think that there is something wrong with *you*.

Yet God says something totally different.

You were created by God Himself (Gen. 1:26). He thought of you before the foundation of the world (Eph. 1:4), and He delights in you (Zeph. 3:17). God loves you so much that He calls you His very own child (1 John 3:1), and He is proud of the steps you have taken toward Him.

The Lord wants to heal you of any lies you've believed about yourself. You are not less than but a valuable, precious child of the living God. Ask Him to give you a picture of who you are in Him.

PRAYER

Lord, I lift up to you any lies I have believed about myself. I ask that you would heal me of thinking things were my fault or that I somehow deserved what happened to me. Give me a picture and a knowledge of who you say that I am and help me to receive your love. I take off condemnation and shame right now, and I lift my face to you. I declare that you love me and that I am beautiful, valuable, and cherished by you, my heavenly Father. In Jesus' name, amen.

DAY 83

Moving On

Set your mind on things above, not on things on the earth.
—Colossians 3:2

There are some things you just never forget.

My friend's great big hug was one of them. I had gone to her for prayer, telling her I just needed healing from everything. I was angry, hurt, and my heart was broken.

She wrapped her arms around me and gave me the biggest hug. Then she said, "I see a picture of you, and the Father is wrapping His arms around you, embracing you, and saying, 'It's time to leave all this behind and move on.'"

I really wanted to move on, but how?

I asked the Lord to help me leave these things behind so I *could* move on. I found that it doesn't happen overnight but is a process that takes time. If we ask our heavenly Father, He will help us and walk us through all of it.

With each thing the Lord healed me from, I found something in common with them all. When we are not walking in healing yet, the enemy will torment our minds with never-ending thoughts about the situation, trying to get us to dwell on it instead of having our focus on God.

Pray over your mind. Bind Satan from harassing and tormenting you with those thoughts and past memories anymore. Forgive those who abused you and break ungodly spiritual soul ties with them.

Every time they come to mind, thank God that this is His battle and not yours. Lift them up to God again, releasing them into His hands. Tell the Lord you trust Him to take those things that are wrong and make them right. Declare that you trust Him to heal and restore your life.

The enemy would like to see you in discouragement and despair by keeping your thoughts on the battle raging around you instead of on Jesus. Lift your eyes up to your heavenly Father and ask Him to help you. Keep refocusing your mind on Jesus. He will help you; you are not alone. Our God is faithful and will answer your cries for help.

PRAYER

Lord, I ask for your help to move on. I break every ungodly spiritual soul tie that is keeping me tied to the past. In the name of Jesus, I bind you, Satan, from tormenting me anymore. Lord Jesus, I choose to forgive those who have hurt me. They are your burden now and not mine, and I refuse to hold on to the offense anymore. I choose to trust you, Lord, to heal these memories, to heal my mind and my heart. Lead me into the restoration you have for me. In Jesus' name, amen.

DAY 84

Who You Really Are

Do not fear, for you will not be ashamed; Neither be disgraced, for you will not be put to shame; For you will forget the shame of your youth.

—Isaiah 54:4

When I arrived to my first day of Bible college, the first thing we did was have chapel. After a time of worship, they called the new students forward to be prayed for.

A man from the college stepped up to me, placed his hands on my head, and prayed. "That's not who you are anymore! When He looks at you, He sees the righteousness of Jesus Christ!"

Tears came to my eyes.

I had been grieving decisions I made as a young adult. And to make it worse, there were people in my life who refused to let those things go. Every time I saw them, they were sure to remind me of my past mistakes.

"That's not who you are anymore!" changed the way I viewed myself. I held onto that truth and did not let it go.

One day, when someone tried to remind me of my past mistakes, I was able to look at them and say, "That's not who I am anymore."

Has the enemy been throwing guilt, shame, and condemnation at you? Has he been using other people to remind you of your past sins? That is not of God.

If you have asked for forgiveness, you are forgiven (1 John 1:9). Those sins have been thrown into the sea of forgetfulness (Micah 7:19). God has washed you white as snow because of the blood of

Jesus Christ (Isa. 1:18). Those sins have been atoned for, and God will not bring them up again (Isa. 43:25).

Your past is not who you are anymore. When God looks at you, He sees the righteousness of Jesus Christ (2 Cor. 5:21).

You are forgiven, loved, and cherished by your heavenly Father. He has a wonderful plan for your life and wants you to move forward. Instead of a garment of guilt and shame, He has a robe of righteousness just for you (Isa. 61:10).

PRAYER

Lord, I thank you that when I confessed my past sins to you, I was forgiven. I receive your forgiveness. I thank you that when you look at me, you see the righteousness of Jesus Christ. Help me, Lord, to see myself as you see me. I choose now to take off the cloak of shame and guilt. I cast it off of me now, and I refuse to wear it again. Shame, I tell you to leave me now. I renounce every agreement I've made with you and break your power over my life. I am not my past. Heavenly Father, I lift my face to you and receive your love and forgiveness. I receive my identity as your precious child. In Jesus' name, amen.

DAY 85

Yours to Keep

Now faith is the substance of things hoped for, the evidence of
things not seen.

—Hebrews 11:1

D oubt was setting in.
God had given me promises, then people would say things
to steal them away. Sometimes I felt so alone in believing the Lord
for His promises to come true. It seemed more people were trying
to talk me *out* of believing God than to believe His Word was true.

It felt like they wanted to steal my hope.

I sat alone in my office with the door closed and let myself cry,
giving free reign to my tears. "God, do you really want to do these
things in my life?"

The moment the words were out; my son came tearing up the
stairs. "Mom! Mom! You need to come outside *right now*!"

Thinking something must be wrong, I quickly wiped my tears
away and ran outside after my son. He stopped in the middle of
the driveway and pointed up into the sky.

There, above my house was a double rainbow. Seconds after I
asked God that question, it appeared above my house, where my
children were outside playing.

To me, it meant God had heard my prayer, and yes, His promises
to me were true. I took a picture of that rainbow and had it enlarged.
It hangs in my living room where I see it every day.

Keep what God has told you in front of your eyes. Keep the special things He does for you in remembrance of some kind. Take a picture or write about it and look at it often.

This world will try to tell you none of what God says is true, or even real. They will tell you not to believe, not to hope, not to have faith.

Don't let them.

Every day, set your eyes on something that reminds you of the promises your heavenly Father has given: a Scripture, a picture, a memory.

Don't ever give up on those promises.

They are yours to keep.

PRAYER

Lord, I choose to forgive those who have mocked my belief in you, those who have tried to talk me out of believing your promises. I bless them, Lord, and lift them up into your hands. They are your burden and not mine. I pray that you would show them who you are. Lord, strengthen and encourage my faith and hope in you. In Jesus' name, amen.

DAY 86

Practice Blessing

Bless those who curse you, and pray for those who spite-
fully use you.

—Luke 6:28

The first time I read about blessing our enemies, it made my skin
crawl! Why would I want to bless someone who had hurt me
so badly, someone who continued to make my life miserable and
seemed happy about it when they succeeded?

Why in the world would I want to *bless* someone like that?

But because God said so, I decided to try it. The first time I did
it my emotions did a flip-flop within me, and through clenched
teeth, I asked God to bless them.

And then I did it again, and it became a little easier.

The next time, too.

After a while, I could bless them and lift them up to God with
hardly any anger at all. In my obedience to bless them, God had
taken the hatred I felt for them away.

And then I realized something. What a great weapon blessing
our enemies is!

The devil would like to keep what they did to you in the
forefront of your mind. He would like to keep you tormented,
reliving the pain and anger over and over again until you become
stuck there, unable to move forward. I believe this is one of the
greatest traps the enemy uses.

173

But what if every time thoughts about this person came to mind, you blessed them instead of letting the thoughts torment you? What a powerful weapon this is, taking away the hatred and anger and asking God to work in this person's life.

So even if it takes all you have to even get the words out, even if you're angrier than you've ever been, practice blessing those who have wronged you and watch what God does in your heart.

PRAYER

Lord Jesus, I choose to bless_____ today. Give _____ what he/she needs, Father. I lift _____ up to you and release her/him into your hands. He/She is your burden and not mine. In Jesus' name, amen.

DAY 87

The Image in the Mirror

I will greatly rejoice in the LORD, my soul shall be joyful in
my God; for he hath clothed me with the garments of salvation, he hath covered me with the robe of righteousness, as a
bridegroom decketh himself with ornaments, and as a bride
adorneth herself with her jewels.

—Isaiah 61:10 KJV

I will never forget that picture. I can still see it plain as day.
In the Spirit while I prayed, I saw a picture of a bride. She was
so beautiful that there were no words to describe. She practically
glowed with beauty.

And that beautiful bride sat in front of a full-length mirror,
looking at herself. Only, what she saw in the mirror was very
different than what she was. She saw a woman dressed in tattered
rags. She was dirty, her hair was a mess, and she looked more like
a forgotten orphan than a beautiful bride.

I was touched with a great sadness at this picture, seeing that
such a beautiful person saw themselves that way. And then, I saw
the truth God revealed to me. I was that woman. That is how I
saw myself.

I saw myself through the ugly words spoken over me by broken
people. I saw myself through the trauma and abuse I had suffered,
through the lie that there must be something wrong with me for

those things to happen. The beauty God had created me to be was hidden by the lies I believed about myself.

I knew that the way I saw myself saddened my heavenly Father, and He wanted to take away those things that caused me to look at myself that way. He wanted to heal my sense of self-worth and help me to see myself as He saw me.

God has created you, too, as a beautiful bride. You glow with the beauty He placed in you. You are precious to Him, a highly valuable treasure.

Take what the Word of God says about you and speak it over yourself. As each lie of the enemy is broken by the Word of God, you will begin to see glimpses of the beauty that you really are.

PRAYER

Lord, I invite you into my heart, into my life. Do your work in me. I ask that you would restore my self-worth. Help me to see myself as you see me and to love myself as you love me. In Jesus' name, amen.

DAY 88

Choose Life

I have set before you life and death, blessing and cursing:
therefore choose life, that both thou and thy seed may live.
—Deuteronomy 30:19 KJV

"You feel ugly inside!" It was as if the man had looked into my soul. "But the Lord is going to dress you up, put earrings in your ears, and a crown upon your head."

Then he said, "Choose life. Choose life."

I hadn't even wanted to go to that conference. I much rather would've stayed home. I was tired, but my friend dragged me along anyway. I'm so glad she did.

I never forgot that man's words. Though they were spoken nearly twenty years ago, I remember them like they were yesterday.

For a long time, I didn't know what *choose life* meant. And then, one day while reading my Bible, I came upon the very same words. "Therefore, choose life, that both thou and thy seed may live."

Through a study of this verse and asking questions of those around me, I learned that *choose life* means choosing God's ways at every opportunity. It means reading the word of God and letting it impact how you live out your life, putting the Word into practice instead of just reading it on the page.

And then I knew what the Lord was speaking to me through that man.

I could have chosen to be hurt and offended for the rest of my life. I could have chosen to be bitter and angry. If I had chosen those things, I would have chosen death: not necessarily a physical death, but a death to spiritual growth in my life, a death to the happiness and healing I so longed for. Never would I have experienced joy; instead I would have been oppressed by the darkness that wrapped itself around me.

You, too, have a choice.

Choose life.

Choose forgiveness and live. Choose to ask God to take the anger and bitterness away. Begin to walk with Him by walking according to the truth of the Word He shows you.

When you choose life, God will unwrap the darkness that has wrapped itself around you, that has tried to choke the life out of you.

You have a choice as I had a choice.

Choose life.

Choose life so that you and your descendants may truly live.

PRAYER

Lord Jesus, I choose life. I ask forgiveness for every time I've chosen to be bitter and offended. Take the bitterness and anger away Lord, come into my heart, and help me truly live. Lead me to your restoration. Speak to me through your Word. I surrender myself to you and ask that you would do a beautiful work in me. In Jesus' name, amen.

DAY 89

A Story

Alana's feet were on soft ground. She took a deep, refreshing breath of damp forest air. *Such a beautiful place! Why have I never been here before?*

"You've never looked for it."

She whirled around at the voice behind her.

"Welcome to my garden." A bearded man in overalls stood near, smiling with a twinkle in his eyes. "It's one of my favorite places to be."

He took a few steps toward a garden bed, "This is one of my favorite flowers." He pointed to a particular rose. It had sparkles of gold amongst the deep pink.

"It's beautiful." She moved closer and bent to take in the flower's enchanting aroma. She could only describe the smell as pure beauty. She ran her finger across the petals, feeling the silkiness.

"Let me show you where it came from." The man motioned for her to follow him and walked to another garden full of weeds with a single rose barely standing up straight among them. The petals were wilted, looking as if they were about to fall to the ground.

"That beautiful rose came from *this* garden?" She looked back at the sparkly rose. She'd much rather be over there.

"There is a great beauty hidden in the most overlooked of flowers. If they were loved and nurtured, their beauty would shine through."

179

"That other flower has gold on it, but this rose is turning brown!"

"The weeds are starving this flower." He ran his fingers down its crinkled leaves. It stood taller at his touch.

He began to dig it out of the ground, his strong hands embracing it gently. "People see this flower and say ugly things about it, even ignore it. That doesn't do the flower any good. But if someone would see that this flower only needs to be nourished, the flower would bud and bloom until it had a breathtaking beauty." He carried the flower to the other garden.

Alana thought it looked tiny and frail in his hands.

He replanted it, his shovel scraping against the soil as he dug, "So many miss the majesty of this flower, because they only look at what it is and not at what it could be. It takes a special person to do that."

The man stood up and wiped the dirt from his hands. Kind eyes stared directly into hers. "Do you feel ugly sometimes, Alana?"

Alana let her mouth drop open.

Without waiting for her answer, he went on, "You are one of the most precious, beautiful flowers in my garden."

Tears came to Alana's eyes and she brushed them away. She looked up to tell the man thank you.

He was gone.

DAY 90

Your Heart's Cry

I have shared with you my heart, things I've gone through and how I reached out to God for healing. I've explained that it is a process with God, and that each day you spend time with Him is a day He works a little more in you.

So today, instead of sharing with you my heart, I want you to share yours with God. Let Him hear your heart's cry. Pour out your heart to God in prayer or on the page. Let the tears fall and invite Him to minister to your heart.

It is the work He does in us that makes us beautiful.

Author's Note

The writing of this book was years in the making. Before it was even a thought in my mind, the Lord Jesus was doing a work in my life. I felt hopeless and afraid I would never be "normal." I was much like the drooping flower Alana saw in the garden. Yet the Lord saw something much different in me. He saw the beauty He could create out of my great big mess.

And He prompted me to let Him.

It is in our surrender to Him, choosing to trust the heavenly Father when we've not been able to trust anyone before, that He begins to do a beautiful work in us.

Even though it may feel that the whole world is against you at times, know that our heavenly Father is for you. If you ask Him, He will bring you through the process of healing. Your healing may look different from mine, but the truths we learn are the same: forgiveness, trust, and learning to let godly people love us when we've been hurt.

We are not just drooping flowers in this world, we are the Lord's creation, and when we let Him, He makes us into something truly beautiful.

Contact Information

To order additional copies of this book, please visit
www.redemption-press.com.
Also available on Amazon.com and BarnesandNoble.com
Or by calling toll free 1-844-2REDEEM.

CPSIA information can be obtained
at www.ICGtesting.com
Printed in the USA
LVOW11s0109080817

544194LV00003B/603/P